15.60

Central City Economic Development

Central City Economic Development

EDITED BY BENJAMIN CHINITZ

Abt Books
Cambridge, Massachusetts

Printed in the United States of America.
Library of Congress Catalog Card Number 78-67847
ISBN: 0-89011-524-9

Contents

Preface

Early in 1977, in the dawn of the Carter Administration, it was evident that the fiscal and economic plight of the big cities would be a major focus of attention. These events unfolded in rapid succession:

The President appointed an Urban Regional Policy Group (URPG) to develop recommendations in time for his first State-of-the Union Message.

The plans for the congressionally mandated White House Conference on Balanced Growth and Economic Development began to take shape.

Community and Economic Development was an early target for the President's Reorganization Project being conducted by OMB and the issue of federal assistance for central city economic development was crucial to their deliberations.

HUD, a city-oriented agency, moved rapidly to orient itself to the challenge of economic revitalization.

EDA, an economic development agency, moved rapidly to focus its resources on cities.

Given its commitment to policy, it was natural that the CSA at SUNY Binghamton should focus its annual fall conference in 1977 on various aspects of Central City Economic Development.

Our goal was to inform the ongoing dialogue with formal papers from noted academic researchers and to create a milieu in which the major participants in the policy process at federal, state, and local levels, could share their views. We succeeded in getting representation from HUD, EDA, the staff of the White House Conference, the National League of Cities—U.S. Conference of Mayors, the Council on Urban Economic Development, the Center for Community Economic Development, the State of Michigan, and the cities of New York and Gary, Indiana.

This volume contains the papers and talks delivered at that conference. The White House Conference was held in late January 1978 and the President finally announced his urban policy in March 1978. But the debate continues and Congress has yet to enact most of the President's recommendations.

The heart of the new urban policy is the recommendations to provide strong incentives to keep and attract private employers back to the central city. This SUNY conference had precisely that focus, and a year later, this volume is equally relevant to the current debate.

My opening paper sets the stage by reviewing trends in employment, unemployment, and fiscal condition of central cities. I see the current dialogue as failing to disentangle these indicators in terms of their policy implications. It would be a mistake to limit our options to stimulate employment by insisting that they also serve the other goals of reduced unemployment and a stronger tax base. Other strategies are seen as more effective in serving those goals.

Harrison and Hill of M.I.T., in the second paper see the pattern of job decline and change in older cities as inimical to the welfare of city workers. Contrasting Baltimore to Denver—two cities chosen for intensive analysis—they see an erosion of job opportunity in the old city which is biased against the blue collar worker.

Melvin Mister of the U.S. Conference of Mayors argues that cities can contribute to national growth but that potential is unrecognized in policymaking circles at the national level. Donna Shalala, Assistant Secretary in the Department of Housing and Urban Development (HUD) stressed the emerging emphasis in her agency on urban as opposed to its traditional preoccupation with housing. She cites HUD's role in the revision of the Community Development Block Grant formula to favor old cities and the key role of the HUD secretary in formulating Carter's urban policy.

George Peterson expounded on a theme which he and his staff at the Urban Institute have successfully pushed into the limelight, namely, the anti-urban bias of many of our tax laws and policies. Victor Hausner, Deputy Assistant Secretary for Planning at the Economic Development Administration (EDA) gave a comprehensive overview of sub-national economic problems and development opportunities and how EDA proposes to respond to these challenges. The role of state government in urban economic development was illustrated by Waino Pihl of Michigan's Department of Commerce.

A highlight of the conference was the address by Richard Hatcher, Mayor of Gary, Indiana. The thrust of his address is reflected in this call: "In my judgment, now is the time for a-1 men and women committed to a better future for the cities of this country to step forward and shape the national debate over affirmative action."

Dale Hiestand of Columbia University calls attention to the heterogeneity of the economic, social and political circumstances of cities and makes a plea for greater attention to these particulars in formulating urban economic development strategies. His paper was followed by a fundamental analysis of market failures which defines the appropriate role for community organizations in urban economic development. That paper was delivered by Stephan Michelson, currently with the Urban Institute, but at the time of the conference, Director of Research of the Center for Community Economic Development.

The Executive Director of the National Council for Urban Economic Development (CUED), James Peterson, reviewed the problems of the cities, the emerging urban policy of the new administration and made a plea for greater emphasis on flexibility in the use of federal funds and on achieving greater cooperation between cities and suburbs, a theme which is fully developed in the final paper by Gail Schwartz of the Academy for Contemporary Problems (formerly of the New York City Planning Commission).

The conference closed with an address by Theodore Lane of the staff of the White House Conference on Balanced Growth and Economic Development in which he discussed plans for this conference. Since that conference is now a matter of history, we have included in this volume, a statement by the Advisory Committee to the conference, summarizing its findings and recommendations.

Benjamin Chinitz

Acknowledgements

Benjamin Surovy and Cheryl Green of the staff of the Center for Social Analysis brilliantly planned and executed the myriad of details associated with the conference. Eileen Sinchaski and Cheryl Green transcribed and typed the manuscript. Alas, I must take the credit or blame for the design of the program and the choice of speakers and participants.

We also want to thank Gerald Duskin of the Office of Economic Research of the Economic Development Administration for his cooperation and our own campus president, Clifford Clark, for sympathetic matching support.

What follows is as faithful a record as we could reconstruct of the proceedings of that conference. That task was discharged with hard work, ingenuity, sound judgment, and dedication by Vivian Carlip of the Department of Economics of the State University of New York at Binghamton.

Trends and Prospects

PART ONE

Toward a National Urban Policy

CHAPTER ONE

Benjamin Chinitz*

The central cities of the U.S. metropolitan areas have, as a group, moved into a period of both absolute and relative decline in demographic and economic terms. Between 1970 and 1975, they experienced an overall loss of population at the rate of 0.6 percent per annum. The number of jobs located in central cities (as a group) has certainly declined, although reliable estimates are only available for specific cities.

This is the third phase in the long history of urbanization in the United States. The first phase, which probably began shortly after the rebels put down their guns in the 1780s, lasted until about the 1920s. During these 13 to 14 decades, central cities grew more rapidly than their surrounding suburbs and hinterlands and faster than the country as a whole. Both foreign and domestic migration streams delivered millions of residents and workers to these cities. Urban densities increased, urban boundaries were pushed out, and many city governments were able to annex territory to enlarge their jurisdictions.

The 1930 census was the first to show the suburban rings growing faster than the central cities, but the latter were still growing (again, as a group) in absolute terms at a fairly healthy clip. This pattern of absolute growth and relative decline marked the second phase of U.S. urbanization and continued for five decades

---

Benjamin Chinitz is Professor of Economics, State University of New York at Binghamton.

up to 1970. With each passing decade since 1940, the absolute gains diminished, and many cities began to register absolute declines in population and employment. During the 1960s some 70 cities lost population; fragmentary data on employment suggest that a large number of cities also experienced substantial job losses in the 1960s.

These demographic and economic erosions in the declining urban areas have generated a sense of urgency because they seem to have led to at least two major urban problems: a relatively high rate of unemployment in the resident labor force and increased fiscal pressure on the governments of central cities. The combination of the two problems poses a threat to the viability of many cities and is therefore seen as a national problem requiring fresh national initiatives and bold solutions.

ECONOMIC PROBLEMS: WORKERS

To assess the impact of a faltering central city economy on the resident labor force, we must first take account of the changing composition of central city populations. The major change is the sharp increase in the nonwhite population, in both absolute and relative terms. In the very latest period for which we have data, 1970-1975, during which aggregate central city population declined by 3.1 percent (1,974,000), the white population declined by 6.8 percent (3,350,000) but the nonwhite population increased by 9.9 percent (1,376,000). The difference in the previous decade, 1960-1970, was even more dramatic. Between 1960 and 1970, the white population of central cities remained virtually constant while the nonwhite population increased by 36.5 percent.

Associated with the relative growth of the nonwhite population, but partly independent of it, has been the downward movement of income in the central cities as compared to the suburbs. Comparisons of median family income, income distributions, and rates of poverty, all show a relative deterioration of the central city *in all regions for all sizes,* but the gap between city and suburbs is greater for whites than for nonwhites. For example, in 1974, the rate of white poverty in central cities was 9.8 percent compared with 6.2 percent in the suburbs, a differential of 58 percent. For the black population the comparable figures were 29.6 percent and 21.9 percent, a differential of 35 percent.

Vincent Barrabba has calculated that central cities have in the aggregate lost $30 billion of income through migration in the period 1970-1974. The people who moved out had a total income of $55 billion, and the people who moved in had a total income of $25 billion.[1]

The unemployment rate of the entire resident labor force of central cities is above the national average and thus has been declining more slowly than the national average in the current recovery. As shown in Table 1, this is true not only for the labor force as a whole but for all its parts—white, nonwhite, male, female, adult, youth. Note that the gap between the U.S. average and that of central cities widens in every category between 1975 and 1976, except for youth.

TABLE 1.   Rates of Unemployment—United States and Central Cities

	1975		1976	
	U.S.	*Central Cities*	*U.S.*	*Central Cities*
Total	8.5	9.6	7.7	9.2
White	7.8	8.4	7.0	7.9
Nonwhite	13.9	14.1	13.1	13.9
Adult males	6.2	8.4	5.4	7.9
Adult females	7.5	8.1	6.8	7.9
Youth	19.9	24.5	19.0	23.4

Source: *Employment and Training Report of the President, 1977.*

Much of the current preoccupation with the urban condition and the quest for new policies has to do with this problem of relatively high unemployment rates in central cities, although the nature and dimensions of the problem are often misrepresented. While the youth unemployment rate is very high in the city, it is also high everywhere. While the nonwhite unemployment rate is very high in the city, it is also high elsewhere. The adult white unemployment rate is also higher in the city than elsewhere and in terms of numbers, it is still the largest group of unemployed in (central) cities. To repeat: the factors which make for relatively high unemployment in cities affect all components of the resident labor force.

Recent fragmentary data for 1975 (a recession year) also show higher unemployment rates for the central city than for the suburbs in Baltimore, Chicago, Cleveland, Detroit, Milwaukee, New York, Philadelphia, and Washington. Surprisingly, there is no significant difference in unemployment rates between city and suburbs for the black labor force in all these cities. Yet there is wide variation in the black/white differential among these cities. In New York City, the black unemployment rate was 11.8 percent compared with 10.2 percent for the whites; in Philadelphia, the respective figures were 16.1 and 6.9 percent.[2]

ECONOMIC PROBLEMS: JOBS

The most systematic data available on job trends in central cities are the data which we have assembled from the four censuses: Manufacturing, Retail, Wholesale, and Selected Services, for the years 1947, 1954, 1958, 1963, 1967, 1972. For each of these four sectors (and for the sum of the four) we have created two indices with a 1947 base. One index measures absolute employment in a given year as compared to 1947. The other index measures the ratio of employment in the central cities to their Standard Metropolitan Statistical Areas (SMSAs) as compared to 1947. The latter index is, therefore, a measure of relative growth and suggests the degree of suburbanization. These indices are available for all central cities, at all the dates cited, for all four sectors, with occasional omissions for reasons of disclosure or noncomparability.

Total employment (i.e., the sum of these four sectors) in 1972 was below 1947 levels in all size cities in the Northeast and in the largest cities (over 1 million) in the North Central region as well as the smallest cities in that region (50,000). Elsewhere, it was above 1947 levels, and in the South and West the indices are in the 200-300 range (see Table 2).

The period 1967-1972 was particularly severe for the larger cities in the Northeast. If 1972 Census data had been available earlier, the fiscal crisis of 1975-1976 could have been anticipated much sooner.

TABLE 2. Employment* in 1972† (1947 = 100) in Central Cities of SMSAs
by Size and Region

	Northeast	North Central	South	West
Over 1,000,000	87	70	–	179
Between 500,000 and 1,000,000	77	114	162	331
Between 250,000 and 500,000	83	120	236	318
Between 100,000 and 250,000	84	137	222	243
Between 50,000 and 100,000	98	123	205	253
Less than 50,000	96	82	–	–

*The sum of Manufacturing, Retail, Wholesale, and Selected Services.
†The unweighted average of the indices for specific areas.

Source: Chinitz

Our data support certain generalizations proposed to "explain" or account for the number of jobs in a given sector, in a given city, at a given date.

1) National factors are important in two respects: a) More rapid national economic growth, as occurred in the interval 1963-1967, will sustain central cities' job levels. In terms of our data, the indices look more favorable. b) A sector, like selected services, which has been growing more rapidly than total employment in the nation as a whole over the whole period, will show more growth in cities. All cities show indices well over 100 for that sector for all time periods.

2) The regional factor is crucial in accounting for the value of the index of absolute employment. Values in the Northeast are depressed, and values in the South and West are favored, without regard to sector or time period.

3) The city size factor is not significant, once the regional factor is controlled.

4) The slow growth of cities relative to suburbs occurs at all time periods, in all sectors, in all regions, in cities of all sizes.

FISCAL PROBLEMS

Central cities have very highly developed public sectors, as measured by expenditures per capita, and the bigger the city, the larger the public sector is as a proportion of total economic activity. In part these high expenditures reflect higher prices paid by local government for labor and other inputs in cities. In part they reflect greater needs for public expenditure, such as the higher crime rates which require more police and the greater numbers of disadvantaged who require more attention from the public sector. In part they reflect a greater desire by cities to redistribute income and to perform other functions through the public sector (such as hospitals in New York City).

Be that as it may, the pressures which give rise to high and increasing expenditures bear little relationship to the rate of economic growth in the city except, perhaps, that when there is heavy competition for workers, wages in the public sector might rise more rapidly. But to offset that, expenditures of a redistributive nature would tend to rise when the economy falters. On balance, then, expenditures have their own momentum. Revenues, on the other hand, do respond briskly to the rate of growth of the private sector. When jobs decrease, revenues from personal income taxes, sales taxes, and even property taxes decline, or at least fail to grow fast enough to keep up with the rate of growth of expenditures.

State and federal aid to cities have, of course, grown, and they now account on average for close to 40 percent of city revenues. However, evidence suggests that even in this regard, there has been a mismatch between needs and resources. For example, Chernick[3] has shown that in the 1960s and early 1970s, the largest central cities suffered in the distribution of federal project aid, compared with cities in the 100,000 – 500,000 range. More recently, the federal government has introduced a countercyclical component to federal aid. All of this is helpful, but the city's dependence on its own tax base is still substantial and given the asymmetry in the behavior of expenditures and revenues in response to economic decline, the potential for fiscal pressure resulting from decline is great.

Other fiscal pressures come from the political fragmentation of urban areas, with the central city often bearing more than its fair share of financing social services. In a recent monograph, "Cities in Trouble," David T. Stanley of the Academy for Contemporary Problems has developed and assembled a number of measures of fiscal pressure and concluded that the cities as of 1976 in the greatest difficulty are: New York, Buffalo, Detroit, Newark, St. Louis, Boston, Cleveland, and Philadelphia.

TOWARD A NATIONAL URBAN POLICY

High unemployment, job losses, and fiscal crises have been at the center of the current ferment in Washington and around the country with respect to the development of new federal policies and programs by the Carter administration. It is generally assumed that the main reason we have so far failed to come up with attractive recommendations is that we do not really know how best to spend federal dollars to resolve these problems. However, a more fundamental problem is that we do not fully appreciate the extent to which the solutions to the fiscal crises, job losses in the private sector, and high unemployment in the resident work force, do *not* overlap. Graphically speaking, if we represent with a circle the set of strategies aimed at each of the problems, the area common to all is relatively small.

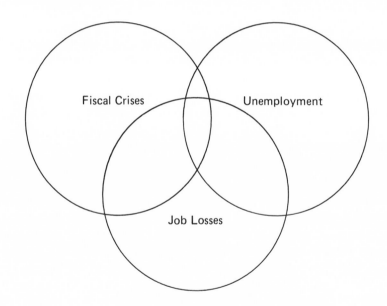

Basically there is only one strategy which will simultaneously serve to relieve fiscal pressure, sustain private sector employment, and reduce unemployment. That strategy is to attract or retain net revenue producing enterprises within the city boundaries with subsidies which require the enterprise to hire unemployed workers who live in the city. It is not the best way to improve the fiscal situation. It is not the best way to improve the job situation. It is not the best way to reduce unemployment. But it is the only way to move against all three problems with one policy.

If we abandon the fiscal goal but try to deal with the other two simultaneously, we get a larger overlap because we can now include a program of wage subsidies to be offered to all enterprises in the city who will employ the unemployed. If we abandon the private sector, we can marry the fiscal goal with the reduction of unemployment goal by a federally funded public employment program, which incidentally also serves to meet some of the public service needs of the city. Finally, if we abandon the unemployed, the strategy set is enlarged to include all possible ways of attracting net revenue producers—enterprises as well as households—to the city or retaining those already in the city.

But if we take these goals one at a time, we have a much richer variety of options. For the fiscal goal:

Shift responsibility for certain functions, for example, welfare and education, to federal and state governments.

Increase the flow of financial support to the city from federal and state governments.

Extend existing mechanisms and invent new mechanisms for sharing the metropolitan tax base more equitably among its constituent jurisdictions.

Strengthen the fiscal base of the city by encouraging the location of more net revenue producing activities (industries and residences) within the city boundaries.

For reduced unemployment rates of the resident labor forces of cities:

Encourage migration to areas where the experience of the resident labor force is more favorable—that is, suburbs and nonmetropolitan areas.

Create jobs in the public sector under CETA and related programs.

Induce the private sector to hire the unemployed in cities by offering firms some kind of wage subsidy.

Provide training for unskilled workers who live in cities so they can better compete for jobs in the metropolitan labor market.

Improve the mobility of city workers so they can better compete for jobs in the metropolitan labor market.

Stimulate the growth of the private sector in or near cities and hope that the additional jobs generated will accrue at least in part to workers who live in the city.

For the job situation:

> Encourage the birth of new enterprises.
> Encourage the expansion of existing enterprises.
> Encourage the in-migration of enterprises.
> Discourage the decline and/or total demise of existing enterprises.
> Discourage the out-migration of enterprises.

The problem remains, however, that we do not yet know how to accomplish any of these at minimum cost. But we can be sure that it will be more difficult if we are constrained to pursue only that strategy which will serve the other goals as well.

The notion that economic development will inevitably reduce unemployment is based on the premise that the high unemployment is caused by the decline of job opportunity in the city. This seems perfectly reasonable, but unfortunately life is not that simple. While there are fewer jobs in the city today than there were yesterday, there are also fewer workers living in the city today than there were yesterday. There are still more jobs than workers in the city, and the ratio of workers to jobs is as favorable today as it was yesterday. The catch is that suburbanites compete for those jobs, and they capture an ever larger proportion of those jobs, as demonstrated in Table 3. Furthermore, city workers *do* commute to the suburbs and in the case of black city workers, they account for an ever larger proportion of jobs held by blacks in the suburbs. The average for ten large cities went from 36.5 percent in 1960 to 52.1 percent in 1970.

Thus, more jobs in the city would not necessarily reduce the unemployment rate of city dwellers, and it is apparently possible to expand job opportunities for some city workers by locating new jobs in the suburbs. Economic development of the city is neither a necessary nor a sufficient strategy to accomplish the goal of reduced unemployment. The jobs have to be targeted to the unemployed, and location is only one variable and not necessarily the most important one in targeting. The occupational and skill mix, provisions for training, and incentives tied to the hiring of the unemployed may be more important considerations.

The natural response to all of this might be, so what? We recognize that we can't hit all three targets with the same dart

TABLE 3. Average Share of City Employment Accounted for
by In-Commuters

| | Males | | Females | |
	1960	1970	1960	1970
White collar	37.8	49.6	26.4	36.7
Blue collar	27.8	39.6	19.6	26.3

Source: Stanback and Knight, *Suburbanization and the City* (Allenheld, Osmune, and
Co.), 1976.

and that's why we want a lot of darts. Aren't you setting up a
straw man? But since resources are inevitably limited, and since
there is considerable variance in the uncertainty associated with
the pursuit of the different goals, it is clear that we need to articulate the importance we attach to each of the goals and that such
an articulation should be central to the development of a national
urban policy.

CITY VERSUS JURISDICTION

In thinking about goals and priorities in urban policy it might be
helpful to compare urban policy to foreign policy. What are the
goals of our foreign policy? To preserve our independence and to
avoid war. Priorities? We will not give up our independence to
avoid war, that is, we will go to war to preserve our independence.
What is the comparable statement for urban policy? The goals of
urban policy are to save our cities, save the city jurisdictions, and
improve the welfare of current residents. Priorities? It seems that
each goal is best pursued by strategies which do not serve the
other goals. But is it also true to some extent that the pursuit of
one goal complicates the pursuit of the other? This is perhaps the
question which has received the least attention. Would it be easier,
for example, to save the city if we gave up the goal of saving the
local jurisdiction? And the reverse: Would it be easier to save the
local jurisdiction if we gave up the goal of saving the city? Would
it be easier to accomplish one or both of these goals if we gave up
the goal of reducing unemployment? Conversely, would it be

easier to reduce unemployment if we could set aside the goals of saving the city and/or saving the local jurisdiction?

To sort all this out we need to step back and examine the causes of our urban difficulties. These fall into four categories. 1) Technological changes in transportation, communication, and production which have greatly diminished the demand for both centrality and high density in the location choices of enterprises and households, except for the victims of poverty and discrimination. 2) The inherited structure of local government in metropolitan areas, i.e., multiple jurisdictions, which translates economic losses and gains fairly directly into fiscal losses and gains within jurisdictional boundaries and further encourages the process of decentralization from city to suburb. 3) Regional shifts which slowed down the industrial growth of cities in the North brought numbers of rural poor to these cities, thus undermining their economic bases and, at the same time, adding to their fiscal burdens. 4) Federal policies which favored rather than retarded decentralization by encouraging low-density industrial and residential developments.

Single jurisdiction metropolitan areas would make the task of saving the city easier because the tendency to decentralize would be weaker and the fiscal resources of the entire metropolitan area would be accessible to public policy. Thus, the pursuit of fiscal viability for the local jurisdiction, which implies prolonging the world of multiple jurisdictions, complicates the task of saving the city. We could go to war—give up the local jurisdiction—as a price for preserving the city.

But if the preservation of the local jurisdiction (unlike the preservation of peace) seems like an arbitrary goal with high opportunity costs, there are two good reasons why it is not summarily abandoned for the sake of saving the city. The first is that the latter goal is very ambiguous and very intangible and, at best, defies quantification. It is not necessarily the case that the urban core has been rendered totally obsolete by affluence and technological change. But it is difficult to define the new equilibrium. Certainly each city will have its own equilibrium, just as each city was unique when cities were still growing and expanding. Just as fiscal viability does not imply any given budget level, so economic viability does not imply any specific level of either jobs or population.

The following approaches a reasonable goal statement with regard to the private economy of the city: **It ought to be our goal to arrest cumulative downward movements in private employment in the city and to strive for an equilibrium level which is not drastically below the historic peak.**

There is a second factor which favors the goal of fiscal viability. Fiscal relief can be delivered with certainty. If federal and state dollars are provided to finance existing city services, then fiscal relief is obtained, thereby diminishing the need to raise taxes. What is then uncertain is the response of private sector location decisions to the improved fiscal position of the city. However, any positive response is a bonus.

When the same dollars are used in the first instance to encourage private sector developments in the city, the uncertainty enters at the first stage. Will the outlays, whether they be for infrastructure or for land assembly, or any other form of inducement, ultimately result in additional jobs or additional residents, and if they do, will they yield net revenue—that is, will the taxes they pay exceed expenditures incurred to meet their service needs?

Thus, in the first case, there is little or no risk that the goal of fiscal viability will be served, and there is a chance that the goal of private sector development will also be served. In the second case, there is risk that neither goal will be served, which makes it hard to defend the allocation of dollars toward economic development at the expense of direct fiscal relief, except for projects which have high probabilities of success. When the chance of failure is high, the alternative of direct fiscal relief becomes more and more attractive.

PEOPLE VERSUS JURISDICTION

It could also be argued that the goal of saving the jurisdiction constrains the pursuit of higher incomes and reduced unemployment for its disadvantaged residents. If the fiscal burdens of inner city poverty and unemployment were more keenly and more directly felt throughout the metropolitan region, there might be greater receptivity to integrative strategies both in the housing market and in the labor market.

But again we confront the asymmetry in risk which favors the jurisdiction. Dollars spent to expand and extend economic opportunity, whether for training and education, direct job creation, or transit services, offer an uncertain return as compared to dollars devoted to direct fiscal relief. However, here the case for favoring direct fiscal relief is weaker for two reasons. To the extent that the money does end up in the hands of the previously unemployed, even if it does not prove to be as remedial as we hoped it would, the loss will not be as great as it is when we invest in economic development and nothing happens. Furthermore, while direct fiscal relief can be a strategy for economic development via the route of tax reduction, it is not a strategy for putting the unemployed in jobs. It is a strategy for putting the city in a stronger fiscal position to cope with the direct and indirect adverse effects of unemployment.

The focus of this paper has been on the goals and interactions of fiscal and economic problems. This is not to say that other urban problems like crime, slums, and air pollution are not central concerns but that their resolution must be seen in the context of a healthy labor market and a viable public sector.

With respect to the fiscal and the economic, three distinguishable goals can be identified: the fiscal viability of the local jurisdiction, the reduction of unemployment in the resident labor force, and equilibrium in the private sector at a level which is consistent with its classical role as a central high-density place, that is, a city. (The latter goal is the hardest to define in a satisfactory way.)

The most cost effective strategies associated with each goal are not identical—far from it. Fiscal viability is best achieved by a restructuring of the public sector. Unemployment reductions are probably best achieved by out-migration, by public employment, and by targeted private employment programs. Economic development within city boundaries is pursued by investments and inducements which are best not constrained by the goal of employing the unemployed.

If we view all dollars as potentially available for fiscal relief, the acceptable level of risk associated with economic development projects should be low since fiscal relief is itself favorable to economic development. We should be more liberal with programs aimed at the unemployed if we can assume at a minimum that the unemployed will receive a large share of the dollars in wages or stipends.

REFERENCES

[1] Barabba, Vincent P., "The National Setting: Regional Shifts, Metropolitan Decline, and Urban Decay," in Sternlieb, George and Hughes, James W., eds., *Post-Industrial America: Metropolitan & Inter-Regional Job Shifts* (New Brunswick: Center for Urban Policy Research, Rutgers University), 1975, pp. 54-55.

[2] U.S. Department of Labor, Bureau of Labor Statistics, "Geographic Profile of Employment and Unemployment, 1975," Report 481, 1977.

[3] Chernick, Howard, "The Economics of Bureaucratic Behavior: An Application to the Allocation of Federal Project Grants." Unpublished doctoral dissertation, University of Pennsylvania, 1976.

The Changing Structure of Jobs in Older and Younger Cities

CHAPTER TWO

Bennett Harrison and Edward Hill*

Since the mid-1960s, an important branch of the urban and regional economics literature has been concerned with the spatial decentralization of employment. According to the conventional wisdom, jobs have been leaving the inner city, exacerbating the poverty and unemployment of the people living there. During the sixties, the focus of the research effort was on the movement to (and the growth of) the suburbs. By far the most important and influential work on this problem was conducted by John Kain and many of his Harvard and National Bureau of Economic Research colleagues.[1] In the seventies, the focus seems to have shifted to the redistribution of jobs among regions, especially from the older Northeast and the North Central areas of the country to the comparatively younger South and Southwest.[2] Discussion of the patterns and consequences of this interregional shift has been a major concern of George Sternlieb and his colleagues at Rutgers University.[3]

During the late 1960s, it was argued that the United States was experiencing a wholesale shift of industrial employment to the suburbs, with retail, wholesale, and service activity following behind. But the empirical work of Kain, et al., upon which so much of the argument was based, inadequately distinguished

*Bennett Harrison is Associate Professor of Economics and Urban Studies, Department of Urban Studies and Planning, MIT. Edward Hill is Doctoral Candidate in the Departments of Urban Studies and Economics at MIT.

between employment variations over time in existing plants, actual plant relocations out of the central city, and the creation of totally new establishments. Moreover, insufficient attention was paid to the effects of the business cycle, to the age of cities in different parts of the country, to the prevalence of civil service and other credential barriers to minority employment in the service sector, or to the growing ability of white workers to move their residences to the suburbs while holding on to their central city jobs.[4] A debate ensued over whether the federal government ought to be pursuing a strategy of "investing in people" (helping impoverished central city residents to leave, in order to follow the jobs) or "investing in place" (redeveloping the central city economy, while providing immediate fiscal substitutes for the lost tax base). That debate has never been settled, either in government or in the academy. This is partially reflected in the continuing inability of the Carter administration to come to grips with the set of urban problems raised repeatedly in the last year by prominent black political leaders in the United States. This is a real handicap, now that the concern over the decentralization of employment has moved beyond the ghetto/central city/suburban field of perception to the larger canvas of the national map.[5]

Three years ago, in a consulting report to the Massachusetts legislature, we began to study the changing structure of that state's economy.[6] At a superficial level, it was easy to see—and to record—the shift from manufacturing to services. But to understand the implications of this shift for employment, unemployment, and local public finance, it was necessary to explore more deeply the structure of the changing economy. Quantitative data were reanalyzed at a sectoral level. Persons actively involved with the process of change were interviewed: employers, union and government officials. The search revealed the progressive disintegration of the middle of the New England economy: those mainly blue-collar, low-to-moderate skilled but relatively high-paying factory jobs that traditionally required little formal education, which willingly took in immigrants, and which offered year-round (as opposed to seasonal) opportunities for work. In Massachusetts (as in the rest of New England), as this sector has declined, those who worked or would have worked in it either move away from the area, find other jobs, or go on relief. Some find work in the region's many small job shops, engaging in electronics assembly, the manufacture of jewelry and paper products, or metal working. But to the extent that the jobs they find are in the low-wage, highly seasonal, mainly service-oriented secondary labor market, even those people who do work are forced to go on the unemployment insurance or welfare rolls from time to time. In Massachusetts, at least, the growth of the primary labor market jobs, for example, in the so-called high technology research and product development sector, has never been sufficient to compensate for the loss of the factory jobs.[7] The situation is made even worse by the generally high "paper credential" requirements which some primary-oriented firms impose as a condition for hire. A structural analysis of the changing base of the Massachusetts economy was the key to understanding who was unemployed, where the unemployment was concentrated, in which sectors (and areas) we could expect to find unemployment in the future, and who would be needing additional financial assistance from the state government. It pointed out—as a purely aggregative analysis could not—that retention (or replacement) of jobs per se may not help local workers' income or relieve local treasuries as much as planners might wish; it depends on what kinds of jobs get retained.

We wonder how generalizable is this model of regional economic decline? Given the rapidly growing interest in Washington in the fashioning of an urban and regional balanced growth policy, the time seems right for a new, more critical look at the pattern and process of interregional employment shifts, a look which builds upon the lessons learned from the suburbanization debate and upon the type of structural analysis which was brought to bear in our study of the Massachusetts economy. In the present paper, the emphasis will be on pattern: a reformulated description of the North-South, Frostbelt-Sunbelt, old cities-new cities job shift since the end of World War II.[8]

We begin by setting forth criteria for re-aggregating standard Census Bureau data in order to facilitate a structural analysis of the changing urban employment base in different sections of the country. The new criteria are then applied to 1970 place-of-work data on ten large cities, to produce a concrete list of predominantly high-wage, full year and predominantly low-wage, part-year industries. This taxonomy is then applied to the ten-city data for the period 1967-1974, with the result evaluated primarily in terms of the differences between the economic base transformations observed in the Northeast and those found in the Southwest. One city is selected from each region as representative; our choices were Baltimore and Denver. For these, we extend the structural analysis back over the entire period dating from the end of World War II. Finally, again for the two representative cities, we conduct an occupational, race, and sex analysis of the changing structures in order to make more detailed inferences about which occupations are growing or declining in demand as of 1970 and who is being affected. (Later, we intend to conduct skill/task analyses of these shifts as well.) The very significant differences between these employment forecasts in the two representative cities underscore the importance to policymakers of asking not only how many jobs are being added or lost in different regions but also what kinds of jobs, for whom, and at what private and social costs.

LABOR MARKET SEGMENTATION AND
THE URBAN INDUSTRIAL BASE

The ideas and categories of analysis that are used in this investigation of the changing structure of urban labor markets were derived from the theory of labor market segmentation (or, as it is often called, dual labor market theory).[9] According to this viewpoint, one segment of the labor market consists of jobs paying non-poverty level wages and benefits, requiring (or imparting) work skills, organized into internal promotion ladders that offer the worker a chance for upward mobility. These jobs tend to be unionized. Workers holding such jobs are able to support their families through their earnings, and they generally pay more to the state in taxes than they consume in social services and transfer payments. The rules of entry into the primary labor market are largely controlled by employers. Those who make good profits, have economic and political power, and are heavily capitalized are able to pay the high wages and to invest in the job-specific human capital of their employees. They often experience real labor shortages, especially for their most highly skilled positions.

The other segment in this stylized model, the secondary labor market, provides jobs that pay low—often poverty level—wages and fewer fringe benefits and require few work skills for successful performance of the job. Workers are seldom unionized, and production processes tend to involve simple, repetitive tasks which most members of the highly elastic supply of untrained labor in the economy can learn quickly and easily. Workers holding such jobs are often unable to support their families out of earnings alone and must therefore turn to supplemental forms of income, thereby contributing to the necessity for high taxation in the state. Anyone may enter this segment of the economy, and young workers typically begin their work careers here. The problem is that many adults are unable to escape from it and spend much or all of their lives there. Employers with large numbers of secondary-type jobs tend to earn low profits themselves and to lack significant economic or political clout. Thus they cannot afford to pay high wages or to invest in the human capital of their employees, and as a result, they experience high turnover. This is not so costly to them as it would be to primary-type employers because of the ready availability of substitute labor, for instance through the free placement services of such public institutions as state Employment Service offices which have (albeit inadvertently) become more or less specialists in recruiting secondary labor.

When the economy is stimulated by increased consumer demand for (say) durable goods or by federal contracts for transportation or military equipment, it is the primary labor market which benefits directly. But this sector tends to be relatively more capital intensive, with complementary high wages (and benefits), so the number of jobs created by any given stimulus is relatively small. The secondary labor market may pick up some small subcontracts as a result of this stimulus, but these seldom amount to much (especially in relation to the large number of workers in this part of the economy). Moreover, the subcontracts to the secondary sector are always first to be shut off in a recession. The increased incomes and consumer spending of primary workers do create jobs for secondary workers. But again, the very large number of the latter holds wages down, and this in turn — combined with the high degree of competition among firms in this sector — diffuses any pressure on employers to upgrade their personnel practices and production organization. The relatively poorer access of secondary-type employers to sources of capital and technical assistance reinforces their inability to acquire the scale and power that would enable them to pay higher wages.

Sometimes, primary labor market employers experience selective manpower shortages. Because of technical (specific skills), "paper" (e.g., school credential), or ascriptive (e.g., race, sex, class) requirements for admission to the primary labor market, these shortages are only partly relieved by the mobility of secondary workers into the primary sector. Instead of using their political influence (not to mention their complete control over their own personnel practices) to reduce these institutional barriers to worker mobility, primary firms often respond to such shortages by importing skilled workers from outside the local economy.[10] Institutional obstacles to the free movement of workers from the secondary to the primary labor market seem to be deeply ingrained in American economic life. A large number of studies has shown that education, training, and geographic relocation are not in themselves sufficient to enable workers to make the transition.[11]

Only some of the variables that theorists have used to define the labor market segments are susceptible of quantification, and of these, many cannot be measured because no public or private agency collects the relevant data.[12] We have selected two measurable characteristics of urban jobs which hold promise for rank-ordering industries: mean hourly earnings and the proportion of employees who work full-time (at least 35 hours per week) and full-year (at least 50 weeks per year). Workers holding jobs in an enterprise belonging to an industry whose overall employment structure is characterized by predominantly high-wage and full-year (full-time) jobs are less likely to need public assistance or other remedial social services and are more likely to be able to contribute to the property and income tax bases of their communities.

The Census Bureau tabulates private place-of-work employment data by county. In seven places, the central city is also a county (or counties): Baltimore, Denver, New Orleans, New York, Philadelphia, St. Louis, and San Francisco, but all the other big cities in the United States are parts of counties, so county data include economic activity located outside the city limits. This disparity is especially great in most of the Sunbelt. We can, however, safely add three other cities to our sample without seriously jeopardizing the cross-sectional comparability that standard area definitions afford: Albuquerque, San Antonio, and Boston. The data for Albuquerque actually refer to Bernalillo County. Those for San Antonio refer to Bexar County. Boston is a part of Suffolk County. In the first two places, there appear to be no important industrial districts outside the city. In the case of Boston the other towns within Suffolk County (Chelsea, Winthrop, and Revere) are very small and have economic structures similar to that of Boston itself.

We start with an analysis of earnings in the ten urban areas. The spatial distribution of these ten cities is conducive to our needs in making Northeast-Southwest comparisons. Unfortunately, the largest Southern regional centers, such as Atlanta or Houston, are not included in the sample.

The average hourly wage estimates for all two-digit SIC industry groups in the ten cities for the year 1970 are presented in Table 1.[13,14] These are translated into interindustry rank orderings in Table 2. We correlated each of these individual city rank orderings with the ten-city average rank-order distribution; as shown at the bottom of Table 2, all the correlations were highly significant (a finding that confirms the conclusion set out in footnote 14 below). We then constructed a rank ordering of national industries on the basis of the percent of their 1970 employees who worked year-round at full-time jobs. (Comparable data on a local level are simply not available.) This is displayed in Table 3, along with the adjusted rank ordering of the ten-city mean earnings.[15] These two different indicators of labor market segmentation were also found to be highly intercorrelated.

Thus, we have verified that a rank ordering of industries by their average earnings also reflects the relative amount of work available to a person employed in each industry and that this indicator is stable over a broad range of cities located throughout much of the country. It remains to transform the rank-order indicator into a specific wage cutoff so that we may operationally speak of "predominantly high-wage, full-year" and "predominantly low-wage, part-year" labor market segments. Let us specify the lowest third of the industries in the wage distribution as predominantly low-wage, part-year. This gives us the following working definition of secondary labor market industries:

manufacturing: apparel, lumber, leather, furniture, textiles

nonmanufacturing: retail trade, business services, health services, nongovernmental education services, other services (except legal and professional)

TABLE 1. Estimated Mean Hourly Wages ($) in Ten Central Cities, by Major Industrial Group, 1970*

Industry	SIC Code	Albuquerque†	Baltimore	Boston†	Denver	New Orleans	New York	Philadelphia	St. Louis	San Antonio†	San Francisco	Ten City Mean Wage	Intercity Intraindustry Coefficient of Variation
Contract construction		3.04	3.57	5.17	4.27	3.56	4.63	4.43	4.58	2.60	5.21	4.11	.21
Manufacturing		3.13	3.63	3.67	3.67	3.48	3.60	3.59	3.84	2.66	4.23	3.55	.12
Food & kindred prods.	20	2.80	3.54	3.66	3.48	3.11	3.94	3.66	4.34	D	4.26	3.57	.15
Textile mill prods.	22		2.98	2.66	3.29	2.46	3.15	2.82	2.97	D	2.81	2.89	.09
Apparel & other textiles	23	D	2.56	2.55	2.30	2.22	2.45	2.37	2.47	1.83	2.47	2.36	.10
Lumber & wood prods.	24	3.02	2.70	D	2.61	2.48	3.59	3.16	3.26	2.19	3.81	2.98	.18
Furniture & fixtures	25	2.45	2.86	3.43	2.99	2.41	3.39	2.98	2.97	2.38	4.21	2.99	.18
Paper & allied prods.	26		3.16	3.08	3.30	3.00	3.31	3.32	3.40	3.10	3.81	3.28	.07
Printing & publishing	27	3.27	3.50	4.10	3.74	3.31	4.02	3.66	3.98	2.87	4.39	3.68	.12
Chemicals & allied	28		3.79	3.65	4.52	3.84	4.05	4.55	4.44	2.54	4.23	3.96	.16
Petroleum & coal prods.	29		3.18		3.94	D	4.24	5.22	D	D	D	4.15	.20
Rubber, plastics, N.E.C.	30		3.19	3.64	D	D	2.74	3.54	3.09		3.45	3.28	.10
Leather products	31		2.75	3.17	D		2.64	2.49	2.66	1.93	3.44	2.73	.18
Stone, clay & glass prods.	32	3.41	3.21	3.19	3.95	3.85	3.95	3.39	3.57	2.63	4.59	3.57	.15
Primary metal industry	33		4.22	3.89	3.28	D	3.95	3.77	3.78	2.89	4.10	3.74	.12
Fabricated metals	34	3.09	3.72	4.03	3.39	3.60	3.73	4.04	3.81	3.12	4.05	3.66	.10
Mach. except electrical	35	3.23	4.04	3.89	3.79	4.21	4.05	4.03	3.99	2.80	4.34	3.84	.12
Electrical equip.	36	3.09	4.38	3.47	3.71	2.64	3.57	3.48	3.32	2.42	3.77	3.39	.17
Transportation equip.	37	D	4.40	3.71	4.53	3.89	4.06	4.96	4.22	2.83	5.08	4.19	.16
Instruments	38		3.00	3.57	3.29	3.62	3.54	3.84	3.55	2.59	D	3.38	.12
Trans. & other public util.		3.77	3.71	4.23	4.49	2.99	4.25	3.93	4.44	3.11	4.56	3.95	.14
Wholesale trade		3.39	3.84	4.23	3.98	3.67	4.33	4.12	4.12	3.13	4.70	3.95	.12
Retail trade		1.96	2.13	2.17	2.17	2.08	2.48	2.33	2.40	1.86	2.83	2.24	.13
Fin., ins., real estate		3.07	3.21	3.59	3.31	3.21	3.26	3.51	3.17	2.92	3.85	3.31	.08
Services		3.68	2.53	2.99	2.52	2.29	2.97	2.86	2.61	2.00	3.20	2.77	.17
Business	73		2.12	2.67	2.15	1.88	2.86	2.79	2.45	2.16	3.10	2.46	.17
Health	80	2.34	2.55	2.85	2.47	2.12	3.08	2.59	2.34	2.09	3.31	2.57	.16
Legal	81	2.64	3.10	3.55	3.49	2.75	2.67	3.57	2.77	2.44	4.04	3.10	.17
Education (private)	82	2.44	3.27	3.17	3.08	2.96	3.07	3.67	3.20	2.07	2.47	2.94	.16
Mean wage		3.15	3.23	3.72	3.49	3.04	3.65	3.54	3.61	2.68	3.41	3.41	
Intracity interindustry coefficient of variation ‡		.19	.20	.26	.25	.21	.22	.21	.19	.21	.20	.20	

*Estimated by the formula:

$$\frac{\text{1st quarter 1970 payroll}}{\text{mid-March 1970 weekly employment}} \times 515$$

where 515 is the average working hours per quarter for a full-time equivalent worker (2,060 FTE hours per year).

†For the other seven cities in the table, the city is a county (the data base). For Albuquerque and San Antonio, the county includes the city and a relatively sparsely populated periphery. The other cities in Boston's county are similar to Boston in industrial structure.

‡The coefficient of variation is the ratio of the standard deviation of a distribution to its mean. Thereby its use facilitates a comparison of the relative dispersion of different distribution which is standardized for differences in the scale of the different variables.

Source: U.S. Bureau of the Census, County Business Patterns, 1970. "D" indicates that the data were suppressed to satisfy the disclosure laws.

TABLE 2. Rank Order of Major Industrial Groups in Ten Central Cities, 1970, by Mean Hourly Wage

Industry	SIC Code	Albuquerque	Baltimore	Boston	Denver	New Orleans	New York	Philadelphia	St. Louis	San Antonio	San Francisco	Ten City Average Wage
Food & kindred prods.	20	10	9	8	11	10	19	12*	-3	7*	7	11*
Textile mill prods.	22		19	22	15*	16	18	21	18*		22	21
Apparel & other textiles	23		23	23	22	18	26	25	22	23	24*	25
Lumber & wood prods.	24	9	22		20	15	12	19	14	17	14*	19
Furniture & fixtures	25	12	20	15	19	17	15	20	19*	16	9	18
Paper & allied prods.	26		16	19	14	11	16	18	12	4	15*	15*
Printing & publishing	27	4	10	3	8	8	7	11*	7	8*	5	8
Chemicals & allied	28		6	9	2	4	5*	3	1*	13	8	3
Petroleum & coal prods	29		15		6	3	1	1				2
Rubber, plastics, N.E.C.	30		14	10			22	14	17		17	16*
Leather products	31		21	17*			24	24	21	21	18	23
Stone, clay & glass prods.	32	2	12*	16	5	3	8*	17	10	11	3	10*
Primary metal indus.	33		3	5*	17		9*	9	9	6	10	7
Fabricated metals	34	8*	7	4	12	7	11	5	8	2	11	9
Mach. except electrical	35	5	4	6*	7	1	6*	6	6	10	6	6
Electrical equip.	36	7*	2	14	9	14	13	16	13	15	16	12
Transportation equip.	37		1	7	1	2	4	2	4	9	1	1
Instruments	38		18	12	16*	6	14	8	11	12		13
Trans. & other public util.		1	8	1*	3	11	2	7	2*	3	4	5*
Wholesale trade		3	5	2*	4	5	1	4	5	1	2	4*
Retail trade		15	25	24	23	20	25	26	24	22	21	26
Fin., ins., real estate	73	6	26	11	13	9	17	15	16	5	13	14
Business services	80	16	24	21	24	21	21	22	23	18	20	22
Health services	81	14	20	20	21	19	19	23	25	20	19	24
Legal services	82	11	17	13	10	13	23	13	20	14	12	17
Education (private)		13	11	18*	18	12	20	10	15	19	23*	20
Other services		17	27	25	25	22	27	27	26	24	25	27
Number of industries		17	27	25	25	22	27	27	26	24	25	27
Spearman's rank order correlation coefficient†	†	.90	.89	.87	.89	.87	.92	.91	.93	.78	.87	
Z-score		3.47	4.18	4.20	4.26	4.09	4.67	4.55	4.58	3.64	4.16	

Note: Blank entries reflect zero employment (no firms) or three or fewer firms, the employment data for which is suppressed by the Census Bureau.

*Indicates "ties"

†All are significantly different from zero at the .99 level.

Source: see Table 1.

TABLE 3. Relationship Between Percent of Industry's Employment that is Full-time Full-year (U.S.) with Ten–City Average Wage, 1970

Industry	SIC Code	Percent of Employment, Full-time, Full-year (U.S.)	Full-time, Full-year Rank	Ten City Mean Wage Rank
Food & kindred prods.	20	59	13*	10
Textile mill prods.	22	63	12*	16
Apparel & other textiles	23	49	18	19
Lumber & wood prods.	24	59	14*	14
Furniture & fixtures	25	67	8*	13
Printing & publishing	27	63	11*	7
Chemicals & allied	28	80	1	2
Stone, clay & glass prods.	32	68	7	9
Primary metal industry	33	70	6	6
Fabricated metals	34	67	9	8
Mach. except electrical	35	72	3	5
Electrical equip.	36	71	5*	11
Transportation equip.	37	74	2	1
Trans. & other public util.		71	4	4
Wholesale trade		45	19	3
Retail trade		40	20	20
Fin., ins., real estate		66	10	12
Business services	73	53	17	17
Health services	80	55	15*	18
Education (private)	82	55	16*	15

Number of Industries   20

Spearman Rank Order
   Correlation   .72 (significantly different from zero at the .99 level)

Z – Score   3.13

*Indicates "ties"

Source: Table 2 and *Employment and Training Report of the President: 1977*, Table B–17: "Percent of Persons with Work Experience During the Year Who Worked Year Round at Full-Time Jobs, by Industrial Group and Class of Worker of Longest Job, 1965–1975," p. 215.

and the predominantly high-wage, full-year segment then includes:

manufacturing: food, printing and publishing, chemicals, petroleum and coal, rubber and plastics, stone and glass, primary and fabricated metals, machinery, electrical equipment, transportation equipment, instruments

nonmanufacturing: transportation services, utilities, wholesale trade, finance, insurance, real estate, legal services, professional services

For the set of ten cities, the low-wage, part-year industries all paid mean hourly earnings below $3.00 (in 1970), or nearly twice the national legal minimum wage. This cutoff turns out not to be so arbitrary as might have been thought, for only two of the 20 industries reporting on the percentage of full-time, full-year work show more year-round work than our taxonomy would predict: furniture and textiles. This probably reflects the fact that these are mainly rural-based industries, which have come to constitute an important—albeit low paying—part of the economic bases of many rural areas. In urban places, however, they are much less important, and the amount of year-round work they provide there is much smaller. In any case, for 18 of 20 industries, the $3.00/hour cutoff appears to be appropriate.

URBAN ECONOMIC BASE
TRANSFORMATIONS SINCE 1967

Using the categories developed above (predominantly high-wage, year-round jobs: manufacturing industries, nonmanufacturing industries; and predominantly low-wage, part-year jobs: manufacturing industries, nonmanufacturing industries), we turn now to an examination of the structural changes that have taken place since 1967 in the ten cities in our sample. From the earlier debate on suburbanization, it seems important to array the data in such a way as to account explicitly for differential effects of the national business cycle on older and younger areas. It has been hypothesized that, during recessions, rundowns in capacity and/or actual disinvestment will occur first in places where the capital stock is the relatively least productive and where the external diseconomies of agglomeration (crowding, pollution, etc.) are the greatest, so that places with older capital tend to fall farther and farther behind the places with younger capital with each recession.[16]

We therefore organized the post-1967 data into two periods: 1967-1970 and 1970-1974. The first covers the last phase of the Vietnam "boom," while the latter begins at the bottom of the

first of the two recent recessions. Percentage changes in employment during each period are shown in Table 4, along with the
actual 1967-1974 net changes, to give the reader an idea of the
scale of the transformations. Unfortunately, these net change data
partly obscure the underlying processes, especially how much of
the change is associated with actual plant (or office, or store)
relocations and how much is cyclical variation in employment
in enterprises that did not change location at all. As was pointed
out in the context of the suburbanization debate,[17] net Census-
type job change data do not automatically imply the former but
are instead reflective of some mix of the two (along with births
and deaths of enterprises that do not involve relocation, either).
Tabulations of Dun and Bradstreet enterprise data by state for the
period 1970-1972, prepared by David Birch and his colleagues at
the MIT-Harvard Joint Center for Urban Studies, reveal that less
than 1 percent of any state's net employment change in any one
year is associated with the arrival or departure of a plant; all the
rest is the result of births, bankruptcies, expansions, or contrac-
tions in place.[18] In our own time series, we have tried to account
for the cyclical effect through our choice of time period end
points, but our success can at best be limited. Future research on
this topic will have to be based upon enterprise-specific (gross
flows) information if it is to be really useful.

   As is commonly understood, overall job losses have been concentrated in the older cities of the Frostbelt, stretching from St.

TABLE 4.   Changes in Private Employment in Ten Central Cities, 1967-1974

	Total	High-wage Full-time, Full-year[†] Mfg.	High-wage Full-time, Full-year[†] Nonmfg.	Low-wage Part-year* Mfg.	Low-wage Part-year* Nonmfg.[†]
Albuquerque					
1967–1974 net change	35056	4756	6461	1855	15954
1967–1974 % change	12	18	7	8	13
1970–1974 % change	33	43	29	175	42
Baltimore					
1967–1974 net change	-36290	-13988	-9349	-10530	466
1967–1970 % change	0	-6	2	-17	6
1970–1974 % change	-10	-10	-12	-40	-5

Table 4   Con't.

	Total	High-wage Full-time, Full-year[†]		Low-wage Part-year*	
		Mfg.	Nonmfg.	Mfg.	Nonmfg.[†]
Boston					
1967–1974 net change	−14671	−21007	35	−10850	8002
1967–1970 % change	6	−6	9	−21	10
1970–1974 % change	−9	−26	−8	−30	−5
Denver					
1967–1974 net change	53814	8030	19808	112	21753
1967–1970 % change	15	15	15	21	13
1970–1974 % change	8	5	10	−14	10
New Orleans					
1967–1974 net change	−12538	−10356	−5412	−877	8317
1967–1970 % change	−1	−19	4	5	5
1970–1974 % change	−4	−16	−7	−20	4
New York					
1967–1974 net change	−222181	−117675	−13888	−97230	−7351
1967–1970 % change	4	−1	8	−9	7
1970–1974 % change	−11	−20	−9	−21	−7
Philadelphia					
1967–1974 net change	−69327	−62253	−1877	−2208	10142
1967–1970 % change	0	−8	5	−10	6
1970–1974 % change	−9	−23	−5	−32	4
St. Louis					
1967–1974 net change	−44277	−3653	−19683	−6012	−9793
1967–1970 % change	0	−2	2	−16	−13
1970–1974 % change	−11	−1	−20	−16	−13
San Antonio					
1967–1970 net change	68518	6906	13086	1460	32518
1967–1970 % change	16	25	14	30	17
1970–1974 % change	23	7	18	−2	21
San Francisco					
1967–1974 net change	74619	−8664	45888	1523	16574
1967–1970 % change	5	−27	5	15	9
1970–1974 % change	14	−15	23	1	3

Source: U.S. Bureau of the Census, *County Business Patterns,* 1967, 1970, 1974.

*Includes textile (SIC 22), apparel (SIC 23), lumber (SIC 24), furniture (SIC 25), and leather (SIC 31); retail trade, business services, health services, private educational services (SIC 73, 80, 82), and other services except legal and professional.

†Does not include government or construction employment.

Louis to Boston, and even include the older areas of the South (represented here by New Orleans) and the West (San Francisco). Conversely, in the Southwest employment has grown fairly steadily, even (with a few exceptions) through the 1969-1970 recession.

The data on individual labor market segments allowed us to examine hypotheses about the true nature of the job problem in both sets of cities. In the older cities, where both high- and low-wage manufacturing were generally declining throughout the 1967-1974 period, the pattern for the nonmanufacturing industries depended to a far greater extent on the business cycle. Transportation, communications, utilities, wholesale trade, and legal services, which made up the bulk of the high-wage, full-year nonmanufacturing segment, grew before 1970 then declined (in most places) during and after the recession. The low-wage, part-year nonmanufacturing segment, retail trade and other services, showed a similar pattern, with the rate of growth slowing down (if not actually becoming negative) after 1970.

Over the last 30 years in the United States, as more and more workers have been displaced from the secularly declining manufacturing sector, optimists have pointed to the growth of the service sector as the savior of the city, mainly because service employment was thought to be much less subject to the business cycle than is manufacturing. We already know, from the dual labor market researchers, that services are often more unstable than manufacturing in terms of turnover and seasonality. Now, in Table 4, we see that, in the older areas of the country at least, they have become cyclically unstable as well. Since this is the part of any city's economy which provides the greatest source of jobs for the poor and the nonwhite, there is genuine cause for alarm in these findings. It is true that public service employment, which had absorbed many disadvantaged city workers even before the advent of explicit federal programs, grew rapidly during this period. (It has slowed down considerably since.) But even if we could instantly dismantle those public sector credential barriers to entry which do not reflect genuine skill requirements, the growth of government jobs alone could not possibly meet the needs of all those displaced from private employment. And of course public employment contributes neither business income nor property taxes to a city's treasury.

In the younger cities of the Southwest we see a very different picture. In Denver, Albuquerque, and San Antonio (the only Sunbelt cities for whom detailed and consistent data are available) overall private job growth has been substantial, even into the recession and the post-Vietnam transition. The predominantly high-wage, stable, and often credential-conscious nonmanufacturing firms grew at a fast pace but so did both of the manufacturing segments. Moreover, unlike the older cities, the younger areas experienced explosive growth of employment in the low-wage, part-year services and in retail trade. This is really not surprising, since population has been moving from the older to the younger areas of the country for some time, and these low-wage, high-turnover, often seasonal jobs tend to follow population. (The table does not show another sector which naturally grows faster in newer areas than in older ones: residential, factory, office, and school construction.) But what is most dramatic about these figures is that, in the three southwestern cities in the sample, the business cycle had little or no impact upon the steady growth of the nonmanufacturing labor market segments. Indeed, in some places, growth of these activities actually accelerated during the recession!

Thus we find that the jobs that have traditionally been most readily accessible to the poor are becoming more unstable in the older cities but are growing rapidly (and steadily) in the younger places of the country. This is surely a structural difference of great potential importance.

THE DEVELOPMENT OF THE BALTIMORE
AND DENVER ECONOMIES SINCE 1948:
A STUDY IN CONTRASTS

The impressions formed in the earlier section make it clear that stratification and presentation of urban employment data along the dimensions we have chosen can provide new insight into the nature of economic growth and development. We now want to lengthen the time series and to extend our analysis into additional dimensions: the changing industry mix and the occupational, race, and sex implications of these changes. In order to protect ourselves from information overload during these experimental excursions, we have found it convenient to focus on the changes over time in two places.

Inspection of the raw data underlying the growth rates reported in Table 4 showed that Baltimore and Denver seem reasonably representative of the older and younger cities in our sample of ten. Moreover, they are situated in the two regions of the country which are so often being compared by federal policy makers these days: the Frostbelt and the Sunbelt. Except for topographical limitations along one border (the Atlantic Ocean for Baltimore and the Rocky Mountains to the west of Denver), each sits upon a broad, flat plain which has allowed development to take place ubiquitously in and around the central city. They are roughly comparable in the scale of their private (nonconstruction) employment bases; Baltimore had about 313,000 such jobs located within its municipal borders in 1974, compared with Denver's 253,000 jobs in the same year.

Percentage growth rates for six intervals in the period 1948-1974 are presented in Table 5, together with selected net employment change data. (We had wanted to compare suburban growth in each city, too, but again, the data would not allow it.) In Baltimore, the older city, in the Northeast, we observe a declining trend which has been subject to pronounced business cycles.[19] That is, the change in the supply of jobs periodically grows and declines but always with a tendency toward a shrinkage of the job base. The low-wage, part-year manufacturing sector shows the greatest relative decline over time, as apparel, furniture, and other enterprises in this segment of the labor market cut back on their operations in Baltimore, went out of business, sold out to national corporations, or moved South. (Remember that net change data do not allow us to distinguish among these causes.) High-wage manufacturing received a strong boost from the national economic expansion of the mid-1960s but an even stronger setback from the recession of 1969-1970. Although the low-wage, nonmanufacturing segment experienced continuous positive growth (at least until 1970), this pattern, too, was marked by cyclical changes. Moreover, the swings in employment in retail trade and the low-wage services grew more pronounced over time, so much so that the supply of jobs in this segment actually declined during the early 1970's.

TABLE 5.   Changes in Private Employment in Baltimore and Denver
(Central Cities), 1948–1974, by Labor Market Segment*

	Total Private Employment	Predominantly High-wage, Full-time, Full-year		Predominantly Low-wage Part-year	
		Mfg.	Nonmfg.	Mfg.	Nonmfg.
Baltimore					
Percent change					
1948–1953	5	4	5	10	10
1953–1959	-4	-19	1	-17	15
1959–1962	0	-1	-1	0	3
1962–1967	8	10	2	3	12
1967–1970	0	-5	2	-17	6
1970–1974	-10	-10	-12	-40	-5
Net change					
1948–1962	2,664	-17,235	4,594	-7,029	27,661
1962–1967	27,379	-8,278	1,671	662	15,095
1967–1974	-36,290	-13,988	-9,349	-10,530	466
Denver					
Percent change					
1948–1953	20	21	-23	43	-42
1953–1959	11	1	21	-55	21
1959–1962	12	12	7	5	17
1962–1967	11	2	14	8	14
1967–1970	15	15	15	21	13
1970–1974	9	4	10	-14	10
Net change					
1948–1962	66,190	9,687	-385	-1,434	-16,656
1962–1967	21,875	955	8,725	208	11,390
1967–1974	53,814	8,030	19,808	112	21,753

*For explanation of the aggregation scheme, see Table 4, note *.

Source: U.S. Dept. of Commerce, *County Business Patterns*, 1948, 1953, 1959, 1962, 1967, 1970, 1974.

In Denver, the younger city, in the West-Southwest, we find a very different pattern. Let us ignore the record between 1948 and 1953; these are the years when the U.S. military first closed its extensive training facilities in Denver in the wake of World War II, and then reopened them along with linked production operations during the Korean War. From 1953 into the middle of the 1970s, Denver experienced an upward growth trend in every sector. As in the rest of the United States (including older Baltimore), the manufacturing industries were sensitive to the national business cycle (although the high-wage, full-year job base never actually declined at any time). But the nonmanufacturing industries, whether high- or low-wage, showed virtually no cyclical sensitivity at all. Denver's growth has been steadier than Baltimore's decline. Even in the one labor market segment where Baltimore has undergone long-term positive growth—the low-wage, part-year non-manufacturing industries—the pattern of growth has been unstable, in marked contrast to the year-in-and-year-out steady growth of the corresponding set of jobs in Denver.

The figures we have been discussing describe changes in the components of the economic base from one point in time to another. With each change, the base as a whole may or may not be changing; thus, we want to know what is happening to the sectoral composition, or mix, of employment over time. This is indicated in Table 6 and, once again, the two cities could not be more unlike one another. In Baltimore, the low-wage, part-year nonmanufacturing activities increased their share of the total private employment base from 31 percent in 1953 to 43 percent 20 years later. This growth at the low end of the wage scale came at the expense of all other kinds of jobs.

The extent to which the modern histories of these two representative cities differ can only be appreciated after the findings about cyclical stability (or instability) and changing sectoral/segmental mix are integrated. For at least two decades, through three national recessions, Denver has undergone balanced and cyclically stable economic growth. Baltimore, on the other hand, has experienced uneven and cyclically volatile decline. In Denver, unlike Baltimore, the growth of these jobs seems not to have come at the expense of the development of the primary labor market. We are prepared to infer from this evidence that while the proportion of jobs in the low-wage, part-year nonmanufacturing sector is now the same in both cities, Denver's low-wage service and retail trade jobs seem more reliably available to the nonskilled, disadvantaged, and young workers who tend to need them the most.

What might explain these different developmental patterns in the older and younger cities, as represented here by Baltimore and

TABLE 6.   The Distribution of Employment by Labor Market Segments:
Baltimore and Denver, 1953-1974

Year	Segment		Baltimore	Denver
1953				
	Total private (nonconstruction)	(no.)	327,000	144,000
	High-wage, full-year manufacturing		.32	.23
	High-wage, full-year nonmanufacturing	shares	.29	.34
	Low-wage, part-year manufacturing		.08	.04
	Low-wage, part-year nonmanufacturing		.31	.39
1962				
	Total private (nonconstruction)	(no.)	319,000	184,000
	High-wage, full-year manufacturing		.27	.21
	High, full-year nonmanufacturing	shares	.29	.35
	Low-wage, part-year manufacturing		.06	.01
	Low-wage, part-year nonmanufacturing		.38	.43
1970				
	Total private (nonconstruction)	(no.)	346,000	233,000
	High-wage, full-year manufacturing		.25	.20
	High-wage, full-year nonmanufacturing	shares	.28	.36
	Low-wage, part-year manufacturing		.05	.02
	Low-wage, part-year nonmanufacturing		.41	.44
1974				
	Total private (nonconstruction)	(no.)	313,000	253,000
	High-wage, full-year manufacturing		.25	.19
	High-wage, full-year nonmanufacturing	shares	.27	.36
	Low-wage, part-year manufacturing		.04	.01
	Low-wage, part-year nonmanufacturing		.43	.44

Source: Same as Table 5.

Denver? Why is the older area becoming more vulnerable to the eroding effects of national recessions, both over time and relative to the younger area? Until we have had a chance to assemble and study private and public investment (and disinvestment) data, we can only hazard some guesses. That services are still generally more stable than manufacturing—and that Denver is, like all new cities, heavily stocked with service industries—is a factor which must be taken into account in any comparison (although we have already noted that Baltimore's service industries are themselves becoming more unstable over time). The physical capital stock—housing, industrial and commercial infrastructure, transportation hardware—is younger and presumably more efficient in Denver.

The transport mix and the lower density of the built environment conjoin in Denver to promote conventional ("sprawled") spatial growth. The younger cities are like bottles not yet full, while the older cities like Baltimore have long been spilling over the edges.[20]

One factor which has been the object of much speculation lately, and which we think bears further investigation, is the direct and indirect role of the federal government in the economies of the different area. For example, to what extent might the substantial role of the federal government as consumer of both military and civilian goods and services be helping to balance the economic base of Denver and stabilize its growth over the cycle? Several writers have suggested that a "shelter" from ordinary market competition is often provided to firms and regions when they are intensely involved in federal contracting. It is hypothesized that the shelter provides such firms with a significant measure of monopoly power.[21] To the extent that this is reflected in the growth of the primary labor market in a community, we would expect cities with large numbers of government contractors to offer higher paying and more stable work, relative to cities not so generously endowed with well connected capitalists.

In any case, whatever the causes of the observed structural differences in the economic base transformations in older and younger cities such as Baltimore and Denver, it must surely be the case that different groups of workers face objectively different circumstances in these labor market areas. We shall now turn to an analysis of the patterns of the demand for labor in our two representative cities.

THE OCCUPATIONAL IMPLICATIONS OF THE DIFFERENCES IN INDUSTRIAL STRUCTURE BETWEEN BALTIMORE AND DENVER

As industries grow and decline, employers' demands for specialized labor vary, too. These signals in the labor market largely determine which and how many people will work, where they will work, and how many may have to move out of the area altogether to find jobs elsewhere.

We decided to use the 1970 Census industry-by-occupation tables for the Baltimore and Denver SMSAs to draw inferences about shift in the demand for different occupations over the 1967-1974 period, resulting from the measured changes in the levels and mix of industrial activity. Direct measurement of the occupational distributions in the two cities for the two years was not possible, due to inadequate or unavailable data. While the industry information we have been using refers to place of work (i.e., it is enterprise based), official occupational data come from surveys of households so that they refer to place of residence. Moreover, for individual urban areas (and only metropolitan areas at that, data for central cities are still not available), the only complete source is the 1970 Census of Population. In using this imperfect tool, we are assuming that the 1970 "technology" (labor proportions in the different industries) remains reasonably descriptive of the whole seven-year period.

Table 7 displays the distributions of 1970 occupation employment in terms of our re-aggregation of the industry groups into the four labor market segments. In general, high-wage manufacturing has proportionately more professional, technical, clerical, and crafts workers than low-wage manufacturing, which in turn has relatively more managers and a much larger share of operatives. This suggests to us that the low-wage industries probably innovate less, are involved in fewer fabricating operations, and have much smaller internal bureaucracies than the high-wage, full-year manufacturing sector. High-wage nonmanufacturing differs from the other sectors in terms of the increased role played by clerical and sales workers.

There are some interesting differences between the occupational structures of the low-wage manufacturing sectors in Baltimore and Denver which could be partially due to the differing ages of their physical plants. Denver has a much smaller proportion of operatives and a greater proportion of managers and craftsmen in its low-wage, part-year manufacturing sector than does Baltimore. This may indicate that Denver's low-wage sector is made up of slightly larger firms than in Baltimore, or at least firms that have a more elaborate administrative structure. We verified this hypothesis by referring to the establishment size distributions in *County Business Patterns.* There we learned that the low-wage sector of the Baltimore economy has a larger proportion of small firms, relative to Denver.

We have already seen how dissimilar the changes in the patterns of economic growth in the two cities have been over time.

TABLE 7. Distribution of Employees by Labor Market Segment by Occupation: 1970

	Total	Prof. Technical Kindred	Managers Admini- stration	Sales Workers	Clerical Workers	Craftsmen Kindred	Operatives Except Transport	Transport Operatives	Laborers	Service Workers
Baltimore										
High-wage, full-year, manufacturing	1.0	.11	.04	.03	.13	.25	.33	.04	.05	.02
High-wage, full-year, nonmanufacturing	1.0	.06	.10	.12	.32	.12	.04	.13	.07	.04
Low-wage, part-year, manufacturing	1.0	.03	.04	.03	.11	.13	.60	.02	.03	.01
Low-wage, part-year, nonmanufacturing	1.0	.15	.09	.14	.17	.07	.06	.02	.03	.27
Denver										
High-wage, full-year, manufacturing	1.0	.18	.17	.04	.15	.19	.27	.03	.03	.02
High-wage, full-year, nonmanufacturing	1.0	.08	.13	.14	.32	.11	.03	.10	.04	.04
Low-wage, part-year, manufacturing	1.0	.03	.08	.07	.09	.17	.49	.02	.04	.01
Low-wage, part-year, nonmanufacturing	1.0	.18	.09	.10	.16	.08	.05	.01	.03	.29

Source: U.S. Bureau of the Census of Population: 1970, Vol. 2, *Characteristics of the Population*. Table 180 "Occupations of Employed Persons by Industry Group and Sex: 1970."

TABLE 8. Distribution of Net Employment Change in Baltimore and Denver by Occupation: 1967–1974*

	Total Change	Prof. Technical Kindred	Managers Administration	Sales Workers	Clerical Workers	Craftsmen Kindred	Operatives Except Transport	Transport Operatives	Laborers	Service Workers
Percent change: 1967–1974										
Baltimore										
High-wage, full-year, manufacturing	-15.6	-1.6	-0.7	-0.4	-2.0	-3.9	-5.2	-0.5	-0.9	-0.4
High-wage, full-year, nonmanufacturing	-9.6	-0.6	-1.0	-1.1	-3.1	-1.2	-0.3	-1.2	-0.6	-0.3
Low-wage, full-year, manufacturing	-23.0	-1.5	-2.4	-1.5	-6.4	-7.7	-34.0	-0.9	-1.8	-0.7
Low-wage, full-year, nonmanufacturing	0.7	0.1	0.1	0.1	0.1	0.0	0.0	0.0	0.0	0.2
Denver										
High-wage, full-year, manufacturing	19.3	3.5	1.3	0.8	2.9	3.7	5.2	0.6	0.6	0.4
High-wage, full-year, nonmanufacturing	25.7	2.0	3.3	3.6	8.2	2.8	0.8	2.6	1.0	1.0
Low-wage, full-year, manufacturing	6.7	0.2	0.5	0.4	0.6	1.1	3.4	0.1	0.3	0.1
Low-wage, full-year, nonmanufacturing	22.9	4.1	2.1	2.3	3.7	1.8	1.1	0.2	0.7	6.6
Net change: 1967–1974										
Baltimore										
High-wage, full-year, manufacturing	-13,988	-1,483	-629	-364	-1,818	-3,497	-4,658	-490	-685	-350
High-wage, full-year, nonmanufacturing	9,349	-598	-972	-1,122	-2,982	-1,150	-346	-1,215	-636	-327
Low-wage, full-year, manufacturing	-10,530	-274	-453	-284	-1,190	-1,411	-6,265	-168	-326	-137
Low-wage, full-year, nonmanufacturing	466	70	42	65	79	33	28	9	14	26
Denver										
High-wage, full-year, manufacturing	5,705	1,027	399	228	856	1,084	1,540	171	171	114
High-wage, full-year, nonmanufacturing	19,808	1,585	2,575	2,773	6,339	2,179	594	1,981	792	792
Low-wage, full-year, manufacturing	112	3	9	8	10	19	56	2	5	1
Low-wage, full-year, nonmanufacturing	21,753	3,915	1,958	2,175	3,480	1,740	1,088	217	653	6,308

*Numbers in cells may not add to total change due to rounding error.

Source: Calculated from Tables 5 and 7.

We applied the appropriate industry-occupation tables to the
1967-1974 industry employment change data to estimate the
impacts of these differential growth patterns on the occupational
demand for labor. The results are shown in Table 8.

The core of Baltimore's occupational structure was hardest hit
by employment changes over the 1967-1974 period. Clerks,
craftsmen, and operatives suffered the largest job losses with little
compensating demand from other sectors. In manufacturing, there
was an estimated loss of 19,297 jobs in these key occupational
categories alone. The high-wage, nonmanufacturing sector lost
another 5,693 positions in these occupations, for a total estimated
decline of 24,990 slots. This was "balanced" by a net gain of only
149 positions in the entire low-wage, nonmanufacturing sector!

As we know, Denver's economy grew throughout this period.
In manufacturing, all occupations prospered, but there were
exceptionally strong increases in demand for professional, craft,
and high-wage operative workers. Clerical positions grew by 8.2
percent in the high-wage, nonmanufacturing sector. But the
greatest occupation-specific growth appears to have occurred in
the sectors that offer the greatest employment opportunities to
the working class and the poor. Denver's largest absolute employment increase has been in the low-wage, nonmanufacturing sector.
These 21,753 positions, added during the space of seven years,
provided work for laborers, operatives, service workers, and others
possessing (and needing) only minimal to average skills.

The difference in the impact on Baltimore's and Denver's
economies is striking. Denver is growing in the occupational categories that Baltimore is losing—high-wage and highly skilled blue
collar functions, on the one hand, clerical and laborer positions on
the other. Baltimore, like so many of the older cities of the Frostbelt, has become an increasingly inhospitable place for all but the
most well-educated and well-connected workers in the population.

THE IMPACT OF EMPLOYMENT SHIFTS
ON MINORITY AND WOMEN WORKERS
IN BALTIMORE AND DENVER

Finally, we examine the race and sex composition of these
employment changes in Baltimore and Denver, again over the

period 1967-1974. Table 9 shows the percentage changes by race and sex, for each of the four labor market segments we have been studying. In percentage change terms, in the primary labor market, men appear to be suffering relatively greater losses in Baltimore and experiencing relatively greater gains in Denver than women. The same can be said for white vis-à-vis minority workers. Analogous results could be read for secondary labor market activity.

It seems to us, however, that a better analysis of the distribution of the benefits and burdens of growth and decline can be conducted by asking: does a group experience more than, less than, or just about its proportional share of the gains or losses? That proportional share is shown in Table 10 as each group's share of total labor market segment employment in one year (in this case, 1970). By this indicator, the job losses are distributed fairly equally among all groups in the Baltimore labor force, and the job gains in Denver are also rather equally distributed throughout the population. There are exceptions. For example, in Baltimore women held 58 percent of the secondary labor market jobs in 1970; but during the period 1967-1974, 64 percent of the secondary labor market job losses were sustained by women. In Denver, minority workers in the secondary labor market had 21 percent of the jobs in that segment in 1970 but received only 14 percent of the new jobs during 1967-1974, which can only have led to a slight decline in their share of the base by 1974. Still, we ourselves are surprised by what must in general be called evidence of great stability in the distribution of the benefits and costs of employment growth and decline in these two cities.

This paper constitutes a first step toward the application of the structuralist insights of labor market segmentation theory to the study of interregional growth and development in the United States. The tools of analysis need much refinement, and the coverage must be extended to a far larger sample of places in order to reduce the risk that what we are seeing is mostly idiosyncratic.

Nevertheless, we have learned much in conducting this research, certainly enough to confirm the usefulness of the approach. These exercises convince us that there is an important historical transformation under way which lies beneath the surface of all the political furor over declining vs. growing areas, older and newer regions, and the new war between the states. It is a transformation of which few people seem to be aware, let alone to understand very well. The older areas are definitely undergoing a

TABLE 9. Changes in Employment in Baltimore and Denver by Segment, 1967–1974, by Race and Sex

	Total	Total Male	Total Female	Minority Total	Minority Total	Minority Female
Percent change: 1967–1974						
Baltimore						
High-wage, full-year, manufacturing	-15.6	-12.3	-3.3	-3.1	-2.5	-.6
High-wage, full-year, nonmanufacturing	-9.6	-6.7	-2.9	-2.3	-1.9	-.4
Low-wage, full-year, manufacturing	-23.0	9.0	14.5	5.5	1.6	3.7
Low-wage, full-year, nonmanufacturing	.7	.3	.4	.2	.1	.1
Denver						
High-wage, full-year, manufacturing	19.3	14.9	4.4	2.7	2.1	.6
High-wage, full-year, nonmanufacturing	24.6	16.5	8.1	2.5	1.7	.7
Low-wage, full-year, manufacturing	6.7	3.6	3.1	1.9	1.0	.9
Low-wage, full-year, nonmanufacturing	22.9	10.8	11.5	3.2	1.4	1.8
Net change: 1967–1974						
Baltimore						
High-wage, full-year, manufacturing	-13,988	-11,051	-2,937	-2,978	-2,238	-560
High-wage, full-year, nonmanufacturing	-9,349	-6,544	-2,805	-2,244	-1,870	-374
Low-wage, full-year, manufacturing	-10,530	-4,107	-6,428	-2,527	-737	-1,685
Low-wage, full-year, nonmanufacturing	466	210	256	112	37	75
Denver						
High-wage, full-year, manufacturing	8,030	6,183	1,847	1,124	883	241
High-wage, full-year, nonmanufacturing	19,808	13,271	6,537	1,981	1,387	594
Low-wage, full-year, manufacturing	112	60	52	32	17	16
Low-wage, full-year, nonmanufacturing	21,753	10,224	10,877	3,045	1,305	1,740

TABLE 10.   Race and Sex Shares of Net Employment Changes (1967–1974) and Employment Base (1970) in Baltimore and Denver

City and Segment	Male		Female		Minority	
	Share of Net Changes	Share of Base	Share of Net Changes	Share of Base	Share of Net Changes	Share of Base
Baltimore						
Primary labor market	.75	.75	.25	.25	.22	.22
Secondary labor market	.38	.42	.62	.58	.24	.24
Denver						
Primary labor market	.70	.72	.30	.28	.11	.12
Secondary labor market	.47	.50	.53	.50	.14	.21

qualitatively different *kind* of economic development than the new areas. Why? Who, or, rather, what forces control the process of change? What are the implications of this transformation for employment and income of working people in the different regions? Can and should public policy do anything to promote (or retard) these changes? Is it perhaps doing so already? These are some of the questions to be explored, at many levels and using several methodologies, in our own future work.

In closing, it is interesting to relate our findings to the emerging work on the political economy of urban and regional development, as it is found, for example, in the current work of Al Watkins, Robert Cohen, and especially David Gordon.[22] What we have done, in terms of Gordon's historical categories, is to measure aspects of the crisis in a city (Baltimore) which was developed and designed to meet the needs of industrial capitalists but which is now subject to pressures associated with the era of international corporate and finance capitalism. The new high technology-plus-service cities like Denver display balanced growth because their form is more consistent with their function. In the older cities, like Baltimore, form and function are out of whack. Similar observations were made by Galbraith in his recent British Broadcasting System television program on popular economics. The idea bears much further investigation.

NOTES

The authors are grateful to Faith Alexander and Kathleen Gallagher for research and production assistance.

REFERENCES

[1] The seminal article is still Kain's "The Distribution and Movement of Jobs and Industry," in Wilson, James Q., ed., *The Metropolitan Enigma* (Cambridge: Harvard University Press), 1968. This, and other papers by Kain and his associates, have been reprinted in *Essays on Urban Spatial Structure* (Cambridge: Ballinger), 1976.

[2] The terms "older" and "younger" have been used rather loosely in current policy discussions about regional growth and development. The concept of a city's "age" would seem to have analytic content insofar as it is associated with such factors as the age (and therefore the productivity) of the physical capital stock (private and public), the transportation mix (especially roads versus rails), the availability of adjacent open space available for expansion of economic activity, and the stage of capitalist development (competitive, monopoly, finance) during which the city became an important economic center. Generally the terms seem to be euphemisms for "Frostbelt" and "Sunbelt." With some exceptions, such as New Orleans, the cities of the Northeast and those of the South and West do seem to differ significantly along those dimensions that are correlated with age.

[3] Cf. Sternlieb and Hughes, James W., eds., *Post-Industrial America: Metropolitan Decline and Inter-Regional Job Shifts* (New Brunswick: Center for Urban Policy Research, Rutgers University), 1975.

[4] Cf. Harrison, Bennett, *Urban Economic Development: Suburbanization, Minority Opportunity, and the Condition of the Central City* (Washington, D.C.: The Urban Institute), 1974.

[5] And even beyond. Once the scope of the analysis is broadened to encompass major interregional shifts, it is hard to ignore the importance of the shifting of capital and jobs out of the

country altogether, especially to Latin America and the Far East.

[6] Harrison, Bennett, *The Economic Development of Massachusetts* (Boston: Joint Committee on Commerce and Labor, Commonwealth of Massachusetts), November 1974.

[7] The old mill-based industries in Massachusetts (food processing, leather, textiles, etc.) lost 61,000 jobs between 1960 and 1975. Only 11,000 jobs were added in the high-technology area: electrical machinery, transportation equipment, and so on. But service jobs paying less than $5,800 a year grew by 60 percent, adding 170,000 jobs to the state economic base. These data come from the Massachusetts Division of Employment Security.

[8] In subsequent work, together with several friends, we plan to undertake the study of specific cases of private investment and disinvestment, decisions which lie at the heart of the process of interregional economic base transformation and the associated employment shift.

[9] There is a large and growing theoretical and empirical literature on this subject. The basic ideas are set out in Doeringer, Peter B. and Piore, Michael J., *Internal Labor Markets and Manpower Analysis.* (Lexington: D.C. Heath), 1971; Harrison, Bennett, *Education, Training, and the Urban Ghetto* (Baltimore: The Johns Hopkins Press), 1972, ch. 5; and Edwards, Richard, et al., eds., *Labor Market Segmentation* (Lexington: Lexington Books), 1975.

[10] One large Massachusetts primary firm reported to us that it recruits from as far away as Great Britain, rather than having to accept "undesirable" or "incompetent" workers offered to them by the State Division of Employment Security.

[11] Cf. Harrison, *Education, Training . . . op. cit.;* and Hansen, Niles, *Location Preferences, Migration, and Regional Growth* (New York: Praeger), 1973.

[12] The new National Commission on Employment and Unemployment Statistics has commissioned papers designed to recommend new data needs to the Bureau of Labor Statistics and the Census Bureau. Some of these papers will reflect the concerns of labor market segmentation theorists and others interested in small-area economic problems.

[13] We excluded construction and public employment from the analysis, since both are characterized by exceptional wage-determination mechanisms. "Other (private) services" is not shown in Table I because the coverage was incomplete. (The estimated wages for those categories that were reported, e.g., entertainment and recreation, hotels/motels, were invariably the lowest in each city.)

[14] Note that the variation in the intracity, interindustry wage distributions (measured by the coefficient of variation) is quite small across cities (0.19-0.26), whereas the variation in the intercity, intraindustry wage distributions across industries is much greater (0.07-0.21). We infer that, although individual industry wage *levels* vary from one place to another, *relative* wages (the interindustry wage structure) are highly similar across the country. This is important, for it means that differences in aggregate earnings from one city to another are mainly (although of course not entirely) the result of differences in industry mix. A low-wage industry in Philadelphia is generally a low-wage industry in Albuquerque, too.

[15] The adjustment, a simple monotonic transformation, was necessitated by the fact that the full-time, full-year data were available for only 20 of the 27 industries shown in Tables 1 and 2.

[16] For a review of the arguments and the evidence, see Harrison, *Urban Economic Development,* pp. 20-26.

[17] *Ibid.,* pp. 33-39.

[18] Allaman, Peter and Birch, David, "Components of Employment Change for States, by Industry Group, 1970-1972," Joint Center for Urban Studies of MIT and Harvard University, September 1975, working paper.

[19] In the present version of the table, the period growth rates are not strictly comparable since they refer to intervals of unequal length. But comparisons of average annual rates of change, or even compound rates inferred from the employment levels at the beginning and end of each interval, produce basically the same patterns as those shown in Table 5.

[20] In this connection, we can and should take into account the differential political ability of younger and older cities to

annex their expanding peripheries, thereby retaining tax base (and adding officially counted central city jobs). Some earlier research suggests that this is indeed an important factor in explaining which cities grow and at what measured rates. See Harrison, *Urban Economic Development,* pp. 108-110.

[21] Cf. Galbraith, John Kenneth, *The New Industrial State* (New York: Houghton Mifflin), 1967; and Freedman, Marcia, *Labor Markets: Segments and Shelters* (New York: Universe Books), 1976.

[22] The first published example of this application of Marxist analysis to the study of uneven interregional development in the United States is Gordon, David M., "Capitalism and the Roots of Urban Crisis," in Alcaly, Roger, and Mermelstein, eds., *The Fiscal Crisis of American Cities* (New York: Vintage), 1977.

Cities and National Economic Growth

CHAPTER THREE

Melvin A Mister*

City governments have to play a role in national economic growth. Unfortunately, their role is not properly recognized, in my judgment, at the city level and certainly not at the national level. City unemployment rates are one and one-half or two times the national unemployment rate, and it seems as if city governments can play a more effective role in getting noninflationary economic growth to alter those relationships between national and local unemployment rates. But clearly the cities cannot do it alone. It is important to discuss both money factors as well as policy considerations that could be implemented to bring about some change.

The state and local government sector has grown enormously. In 1954 state and local spending was about 7 percent of gross national product. In 1976, it was 11 percent, a 45 percent increase. City governments are not only spending more of their own money, they are also getting a lot more money from the federal government. As a result of the $6 billion public works legislation of the last couple of years and the present stimulus package, local governments in many cases now have 40 to 70 and in some cases even higher percentages of their local budgets coming from outside of the city. The problem of managing all these federal resources with all of the rules and regulations is an increasing bur-

*Melvin A. Mister is Director, Urban Economic Policy and Financial Management Group, National League of Cities and United States Conference of Mayors.

den on local government. Despite all of this, however, at the national level we do not see much evidence of the important role of city governments in promoting national economic growth. In the President's Economic Report issued by the Council of Economic Advisers, there is not very much about city governments or about state and local governments. The Congress now has its Congressional Budget Office which is attempting to do something about the state and local government role, but there is no requirement in the law that the Office of Management and the Budget and the Congressional Budget Office make an assessment to determine what the impact of federal policies will be on state and local government. So despite some policy recognition of the important role of local government, in fact it is not playing much of a role in national economic policy debates.

President Carter has launched a crash effort to create a national urban policy, and we are judiciously optimistic that this effort may have some benefit. However, there are some reasons for concern. If this policy is to be more than lofty language, it must be reflected in actions. Yet, the Fiscal Year 79 budget process, President Carter's first budget, and the urban policy formation process are on two separate tracks, with different time schedules. Maybe they will get put together at some point and maybe they won't. It certainly seems important that they be integrated. There are certain other critical issues which are outside of this urban policy formation process, such as welfare, energy, tax reform, all being handled separately, on other tracks, and it is up to the White House staff, with the President, to put all of these things together into some coherent policy. For years the Conference of Mayors and the League of Cities have been pointing out the inadvertent, antiurban federal policy, and we are hopeful that this current process will lead to something more than lofty language.

What would be some of the aspects of a federal urban policy which recognized the importance of city governments in promoting national economic growth? One answer would be a different set of goals. We have two budget processes; the Congress determines the federal budget now. They pass the resolutions, they set the marks, they set the spending limits, based on what the President proposes. So it is not just a matter for the Administration, it is a matter for the Congress as well. And yet when we talk about unemployment rates and rates of economic growth, we do not talk about them in a very detailed way. We do not talk about them in terms of cities, or older cities, or younger cities. We do not talk about targets for unemployment rates for different sectors of our economy. We do not have a really detailed format for setting goals. If we are going to recognize the importance of cities and city governments, we have to be specific and we have to collect the data to be so.

However, only a part of the problem is data. There has to be a recognition that cities can play an important role in promoting national economic growth. Many cities are trying to do that from there own standpoint, even though it is seemingly impossible. As a result of the New York City fiscal crisis and the continuing problems of stagflation, city governments have placed a much higher priority on economic affairs. It has become a political issue in cities, and so mayors and city councilmen get elected on the basis of their ability to deal with economic problems of their city government and of their local economies. The result is that cities are more vigorous. Economic development is no longer simply the responsibility of an agency with federal money. More and more cities are putting some of their own money into economic development. During the past year, with some help from the Ford Foundation and the National Science Foundation, a series of meetings were held with the League of Cities and elected local officials to determine what their priorities were in terms of economic policy and financial management. It became clear that the most difficult problem is in relating the city's fiscal condition to the local economy. The officials did feel that not very many people can tell them much about it that they can understand, although they do get a lot of people that produce lofty and very thick reports for them, with lots of tables and charts and diagrams and formulas—all of which is of little value for their economic policy decision-making.

Four different areas were identified which these officials thought needed priority attention. One is the local impact of national social and economic trends. The optimists among us paint one part of that picture, the pessimists another. I am reminded of the old story about whether the glass of water is half full or half empty. We have some mayors who are on the half-full side and some who are on the half-empty side. At any rate, there is a belief among many elected officials that the cities do have some things going for them. One is the postwar baby boom growing up. Another is described by the term, "gentrification," where the gentry, the higher income people, are moving back into some of our cities. We have gentry in Washington now, moving back in and taking over parts of the city. Other positive developments include the concern about environment and the concern about energy conservation. All of these factors give cities, older cities, some comparative advantages.

There are also some people who think that all cities are facing these difficult cycles. Alex Ganz of the Boston Redevelopment Authority, feels that newer cities, even the Sunbelt cities, are going through the same kind of cyclical experience that the older cities have experienced. The largest growth among older suburban jurisdictions took place in the forties and fifties. In the Sunbelt cities growth was in the fifties and sixties while in the seventies we find that several of the Sunbelt cities have had declines in population. This is sort of a rolling situation, but there is no need for us to project the same trends of the past into the future. The changes in demography, the concerns about energy and the environment, the concerns about urban sprawl, the national urban policy which, hopefully, will reflect some of these concerns, could lead us to a different kind of future for cities. It could lead to less urban sprawl. Instead of having the FHA and highways promoting the growth of suburbs, we could have a set of national policies which would favor cities. So trying to marry these demographic and social and economic trends with national policy is essential if cities are to play a constructive role in achieving that noninflationary economic growth.

Mayors and elected officials can probably do more about the management of city government than they can about anything else, and in that area much progress has been made. The cities know that they influence public and private confidence in the community, and they can control where public moneys are spent. They can deal with the rules of the game: zoning, building codes, and so on. They can deal with tax policies locally and can try to put all of these facets together in a way that reflects something that we would like to call a local economic policy.

It is a mistake, I think, to limit the discussion to central cities because in many metropolitan areas there are cities that are not central cities but have central city problems. Hopefully some new definitions, some new categories could be developed to include these problems. Looking at the managerial problems that cities face, we find that many older suburbs may have problems that are very similar to those of some central city in another part of the country. It is only by accident that some of these did not get to be central cities themselves and become part of the rubric here. We have played around with some new definitions of what we ought to consider our problem cases, but I do think that the central city-suburban distinction is not helpful. It clouds one's thinking; it interferes with statistical analysis. It seems clear to me that size does not mean anything; it is not that significant. Yet many people have focused on size as an important factor. In my judgment central city-suburban is a similar category. I do not think it is a very useful distinction any more.

Now, economic development also is a difficult term. Economic development has a lot of definitions. To some people it means a new industrial park, to others it means new or expanded manufacturing business producing a lot of blue collar jobs, to some other people it is a manpower training program. Some people use economic development and real estate development interchangeably so that the building of housing becomes economic development—and it is economic activity, to be sure. But what I am trying to deal with in talking about management by local government is what I would like to call local economic policy. This embraces all of those definitions and more, because it sets the framework in which local economic development programs take place. Policy is a political concern of cities and city governments, and it should set the framework for economic development, community development, manpower, tax assessment, budget planning. According to Webster's, policy is any plan or course of action adopted by a government, political party, business organization, or the like, designed to influence and determine decisions, actions, and other matters. This is what is important to construct in communities, because, in my judgment, until a policy framework is developed and utilized, cities will not be able to play the kind of role of which they are capable, and they will not be able to manage these federal government resources properly and appropriately.

Another important term developed this year is "intergovernmental fiscal relations." This is probably one of the least explored, yet most important, aspects of local economic policies. I have tried to define it. I guess the best illustration of it is an anecdote. In a session with a high-level official in the Treasury Department dealing with the President's proposals for tax reform, representatives from some of the cities were told that there were three objectives of the President's tax reform proposal: simplicity—or simplifying the system—equity, and economic growth. We suggested a fourth consideration for the President's tax reform proposals, namely, their impact on intergovernmental fiscal relations. The federal tax system has a lot of implications for economic affairs in cities, but it seems that the present tax system is biased against cities. At the least, the system ought to be neutral. Preferably it would favor cities and favor policies that promote economic well-being in cities. When the President's proposals were published in *The New York Times* (which is becoming like the *Federal Register* in some ways) we noted the proposal which calls for a tax break for the construction of new plants and equipment. We informed the administration that this is exactly the kind of policy proposal that doesn't help cities. Subsequently I think that appeared in the *Times.* (I didn't see it, but I was at a meeting the other day and someone there on the Domestic Council staff said, "There's Joe Doaks over there; he's now our correspondent for the *Times.* He writes memos to the President that get published in the *Times.*") At least the objection was taken up and some people in the Administration did try to make certain adjustments and stress the point that if the tax system is not treated appropriately as far as investment in plants and equipment goes—where cities are put at a disadvantage—the benefits of a lot of the grant programs for cities may be just washed away. So intergovernmental fiscal relations is a very critical issue, but unfortunately we do not get very much attention to it at the federal level.

There are some cities that are groping in the direction of effective local economic policies by taking into account the local impact of social and economic trends, government policy at all levels, improved management, and including intergovernmental fiscal relations. Some of these mayors are telling President Carter that this is what they are doing. Mayor Coleman Young of Detroit has talked to the President about what he is doing in Detroit. They appointed an Economic Growth Council about a year ago, and the former chairman of General Motors and the former chairman of the Chrysler Motor Car Company headed a blue ribbon panel. They have now made their recommendations about what ought to be done in Detroit. They want to create a city-wide, public-private partnership to implement the strategy. The Detroit Council hired the National Council for Urban Economic Development to analyze and report on their whole system, and they paid for this with local money, through their regular budget. Also in terms of intergovernmental relations, Coleman Young persuaded the state legislature in Michigan to pass a law giving $30 million a year to Detroit, a so-called equity package, on the grounds that the City of Detroit, the Detroit Museum, and other institutions provide a lot of services for suburbanites. In negotiating with the other jurisdictions in that area Coleman Young has a very important tool. He supplies water to a large portion of residents in the State of Michigan. So when he sits down with the Council of Governments and tries to negotiate about transportation or water pollution he can act very forcefully to get what he wants.

What I am getting at is that here is at least one elected official for whom economic affairs is an important political part of his administration. It is no longer put off in the corner somewhere with an economic development staff paid for by EDA with very little political or public support. Mayor Kevin White of Boston has discussed with the President the Boston Plan. It proposes 72 projects in four target neighborhoods that require $500 million in public and private investment over a five-year period. If the plan is successful, it will produce 14,000 jobs. They hope to get half of them to reduce unemployment to 8 percent. But this is not to say that these two communities have gotten it all together yet. My only point is that there are things that local governments can do and increasingly they are interested in doing, if they can get the right kind of support in terms of information and data to make those tough decisions.

Those decisions are not only tough, they are politically difficult, and they involve a lot of important public decision-making. One of the most important elements of that decision-making has to do with the so-called public-private partnership. In my mind, the most critical issue is, is the city giving the store away? What is it getting in return? What is the public benefit? How can it be measured? Well, it is very hard to measure exactly what is happening because each community has such a different tax structure.

Any kind of job varies enormously from city to city in terms of fiscal benefit to that city corporation, depending on the nature of its taxing system. Most cities do not have the kind of analytical capability that is needed for the political decision-maker to make those judgments. Usually the mayor is in a position where he either gets this nice development in one area or he does not get it at all. He never is in a position where he can have enough information to make judgments about what he might do to get some extra benefits for another area—at least the kind of information that he can understand and that he can interpret and translate into a political decision. Now these communities that I mentioned, like Boston and Detroit—and there are others—are making early efforts to implement local economic policy, and they are significant because they have political shifts riding on them and they represent movement beyond what I like to call "projectitis," where you do a project here and you do a project there. They also reflect more realism in city planning than do the overall economic development plans that must be submitted for designation as development areas qualifying for EDA grants.

I have two more points to make—one about the national economy and one about what I think we ought to try to encourage in all these cities around the country. For a large part of this year federal economic policy has been reminiscent of *Waiting for Godot*. We have been waiting for this increase in private capital spending. We have been doing everything possible to encourage it. We have been saying we are for business confidence; we have been saying, let us not have a tax cut: we had that tax cut in the plan originally and we took it out because that was going to give business confidence. Well, Godot never showed up. My point is that city governments can play an important role in increasing capital spending of all types. In some ways, at least as I understand economics, if you need capital spending it can be government, it can be mixed, or it can be purely private. We know there is a lot of potential for public capital spending. But I do not think we need to rely solely on that, and I do not think we should. It seems to me that there is a whole range of activities in what I would like to call "mixed-sector investments." We have to do something about public transportation; we need to build 5,000-6,000 busses a year. That's a lot of capital. We need to improve our water. We need to build a lot of waste-water treatment facilities. We need to clean up the air. There are a lot of areas which are a public-private, sort of mixed sector, where the private sector is not doing it all, where the public is not doing it all, but where action by local government is critical in order to make it happen. It seems to me that those demands are clear. There is no reason for us to be playing this "waiting for Godot" game, it seems to me, if what we are concerned about is stimulating capital investment.

My last point has to do with the importance of trying to create at the local level the capacity to engage in local economic policy making, so that we can get some local political clout behind these efforts to improve local economies. I remember back in 1962 when there was no MDTA, and we were completely dependent on the state employment services to deal with manpower. A lot of people started talking about the need for local manpower agencies. Now we have these prime sponsors—they aren't the perfect answer but they have made a real difference in terms of local government involvement in manpower planning and programming. I think we need something analogous in terms of local economic policy making. It is a more political question than the manpower one because it requires that local economic policy be reflected in the local budgets of the communities, so they do have the political clout and the politics of the community behind them and so that they do build and blend together, in a managerial sense, all of the federal and local moneys and priorities and taxes and all of that. In the old days, mayors were concerned largely with only picking up the garbage, catching crooks, and putting out fires. Today's mayors are responsible for manpower, public transportation, eradicating poverty, housing and community development, and other national problems concentrated in cities. Many mayors do not want to get into this economic policy thing. They are being forced into it even though they feel that they have enough on their agenda. How much more can they take on? But politically it is inescapable, and my hope is that the urban economic experts recognize these problems and deal not only with particular projects and how to make them work but help by giving the necessary information to make those difficult political public policy decisions. Some of them are just decisions to talk to the federal government about how to stimulate the economy—not only to the Administration but to Congress as well. Do not overlook the Congressional budget process. It is terribly important. They set the goals. They determine the level of expenditures based on the President's proposals, and each year they have been more liberal than the past three administrations have been, in terms of their targets, in terms of their spending levels, in terms of their economic development activities. So it is important to deal with both.

Urban Is Our Middle Name: New Strategies for HUD

CHAPTER FOUR

Donna E. Shalala*

In their introduction to *The Urban Predicament,* William Gorham and Nathan Glazer note a change in mood with respect to our abilities to address urban problems: "Confidence in our ability to frame solutions," they tell us, "has declined as understanding of these problems has grown. . . . We now know more than we did, but, deprived of our hubris, [we] are less confident in our ability to shape a future as we will."

The theme as echoed in official Washington is somewhat different, but it also stresses the limits of what the federal government can do. *The New York Times* recently reported that "the underlying philosophy is that Federal dollars . . . can have only a marginal impact on reversing the urban decay produced by the powerful economic and demographic trends that have drained cities . . . ."

Although I have my own strong views of how this philosophy should shape the federal role, it is important to note that *just because the federal government does not think it is easy to win, it does not mean that it is not going to play the game.* For at the very same time that this low-key view of urban policy is emerging in academia and in Washington, the federal government is in the process of shaping a new urban policy. HUD Secretary Patricia Roberts Harris is taking a central role in the process. HUD is

Donna E. Shalala is Assistant Secretary for Policy Development and Research, Department of Housing and Urban Development.

emerging as more than just a housing agency; it is becoming an urban-focused agency. We are beginning to live up to our middle name: Housing and *Urban* Development.

This new role should not be interpreted as a signal that we are downgrading our housing programs. Indeed, my colleague Lawrence Simons, the talented Assistant Secretary for Housing, is the Department's most articulate spokesperson for a strategy that emphasizes housing as a major tool of urban development.

It originally appeared that the new administration would emphasize national policies with urban impacts, such as welfare reform and aid to the educationally disadvantaged, rather than designing programs and policies specifically targeted at distressed cities and regions. But that has changed, perhaps because of the recognition that a single approach could not address the needs of these areas in a very efficient way. Now the White House is formulating an explicit urban policy which focuses directly on cities and regions having serious economic and fiscal problems, and HUD has been given a lead role in the formulation of this urban policy.

Because many federal agencies design policies that have an urban impact—sometimes positive, sometimes negative—the new administration decided to bring together representatives from the relevant agencies, HUD, Labor, Commerce, Treasury, and HEW, to form the Urban and Regional Policy Group, charged with the responsibility for making specific policy proposals to the White House. HUD Secretary Patricia Harris is the group's chairperson, with the title "urban convenor."

Part of HUD's role within this group is to serve as an urban advocate. For example, we have already been asked to submit to the White House a statement about the urban impact of the tax reform proposals, and we are in the process of framing a general format for evaluating the urban impact of federal policies.

Although it may seem a trivial accomplishment for HUD to produce an urban impact analysis of major legislative packages of other agencies, it is a significant step in developing our role as an urban agency. No other federal agency has as its primary concern the well-being of urban areas. At best, the policies of many of the agencies are coincidentally beneficial to the cities—and at worst (at least in the past), seriously biased against them. As a result of HUD's new responsibility, the federal role toward cities will be concerned not only with reducing implicit anticity biases in other programs but also with developing programs whose prime objective is to aid urban areas.

A number of the new policies and programs are in varying stages of the policy process, from proposal to implementation. But all are explicitly targeted to needy metropolitan areas. While targeting creates problems — those of choosing the appropriate eligibility criteria or formula and of having these criteria survive the political process without being diluted — the emphasis on targeting aid to jurisdictions, and to projects within eligible jurisdictions, is potentially the most efficient approach to reaching troubled cities.

It is noteworthy that one of the few policies which was relatively effective at targeting moneys to central cities was the recently expired countercyclical revenue sharing program. Under it, aid was distributed on the basis of absolute levels of unemployment, a moderately good indicator of long-term decline, rather than on the basis of cyclical changes in unemployment rates. (Of course, the effectiveness of this program as an aid to secularly rather than cyclically distressed areas came as no surprise to its advocates, although certain members of Congress believe that the wool had been pulled over their eyes on this one.)

In the past, there was not sufficient political support to harness federal resources to the ailing cities except in the context of increasing resources to all jurisdictions. General revenue sharing and community development block grants are cases in point. Analysts have suggested, for example, that central cities may be relatively worse off than they were without general revenue sharing because sharing may have given a·comparative advantage to healthier suburbs, metropolitan areas, and regions. Furthermore, general revenue sharing coincided with the decline in categorical aid which focused more directly on the central cities. Sole reliance on block grants, on the other hand, actually made some central cities absolutely worse off than they had been under the previous scheme of categorical grants because of the phase-down of the "hold harmless" provisions of the original formula. Central cities had received approximately 70 percent of the categorical funds; after the phase-down, they would have received only 42 percent of the funds.

Under the just revised approach, which will overcome the anticity bias of the original block grant formula, HUD will be implementing a dual formula in which a community may choose to receive its allocation based on either the original formula or a new formula which takes into account two additional considerations: the age of the housing stock and "growth lag." (Growth lag, which is a measure of population decline, is defined as the amount of population a city or county would have had *in addition to its current level* if it had grown since 1960 at a rate equal to that of the average of all metro cities.)

The use of the dual formula will increase allocations to major central cities such as New York, Baltimore, Philadelphia, Atlanta, and Denver. But the greatest number of gainers, in absolute and percentage terms, are smaller cities like Yonkers, Bayonne, Pontiac, and Berkeley—cities that in the past decade have been undergoing the problems common to the large central cities. Cleveland, Buffalo, Detroit, and St. Louis will make the most substantial gains (more than 100 percent increase in their capita allocations), while New York, Newark, Baltimore, and Washington will make smaller but substantial percentage gains.

HUD's experience in revising the block grant allocation formula has served as a guide in our current efforts to develop eligibility criteria for the new action grants program. This program is the cornerstone of the 1977 Housing and Urban Development Act, which is now law. It is funded at $400 million for the first year. Unlike block grants, a jurisdiction must apply for an action grant, and the only jurisdictions that may apply are those in cities and urban counties determined eligible by HUD.

The action grants program is predicated on the assumption that one way to aid stagnating economies is to encourage private investment. The grants will provide communities with "up-front" money to help them capture and leverage private investment when it is "live"—that is, when it is ready to be committed. They are not available for project planning for purely speculative ventures that only anticipate private sector participation.

We are well aware of the need to overcome the "myth of the return of manufacturing" in assisting distressed cities. HUD's action grants and community development block grant moneys, together with moneys from the new Economic Development Administration program of the Department of Commerce, must be used to stimulate all aspects of the cities' economic bases. Focusing federal policy on the narrow approach of increasing incentives to private investment solely in the traditional areas—in particular in manufacturing—is dangerously single minded. It reminds me of the advice given to a still-young friend of mine by her doctor: "After 26 it's all downhill, and about all you can do is arrest the rate of decline."

It is one thing to acknowledge that the forces leading to decline of cities and regions are powerful and that the federal government cannot reverse them. It is quite another to assume that the sole solution is to work at the margin to bring back the kinds of firms that have left, or to discourage other firms from leaving. The problem with this approach is that it looks too narrowly at the causes of city and regional decline, and therefore too narrowly at the possible remedial actions. Moreover, it makes no attempt to look toward the future of cities and to a change in their economic function. It merely tries to shore up a crumbling past. As I shall discuss in a moment, we need to take into account the changing economic functions of cities.

We are all familiar with the love/hate relationship between the older cities and technology. In the early days these cities were nourished by manufacturing. But as transportation and production techniques changed, as the cities grew old and economies turned to diseconomies, the exodus began. Families left in search of space and other amenities, and firms left in pursuit of new production techniques and cheaper or more convenient labor sources. First they abandoned the central cities for the suburbs, and eventually they abandoned the older regions for the South and West (with a good bit of help from federal policy). When that happened, the plight of the older Northeast and North Central cities was compounded. For following in the wake of these trends came not only an impacted poor population and the externalities of poverty, crime and poor schools, but also starved municipal treasuries facing rising costs and declining revenues.

Manufacturing once nourished cities such as New York and Philadelphia, Baltimore and Detroit. But today, to attempt to stimulate manufacturing in the declining areas is surely pushing a boulder uphill. Lest there be any doubt, the latest data from the 1975 Census of Manufactures hammer the point home once again: manufacturing is not the wave of the future for cities. In the three-year period 1972-1975, central cities lost almost as many manufacturing jobs as in all of the previous nine years, 1963-1972. (In a sample of 56 cities, 208,000 jobs were lost in the three-year span and 237,000 were lost in the earlier nine-year span—a decline of about 9 percent in each of the two periods.) Incremental subsidies will not reverse a trend of this duration or magnitude.

What might we better do? In formulating policy we should heed the following points:

1) Manufacturing is the past, not the future, of older central cities. I want to be careful here, because manufacturing is still a significant factor in the economies of many older cities, and cities still need help to retain and, if the opportunity presents itself, to marginally expand what manufacturing they have. However, to encourage economic development in the city, we should look to the future for something in which the city can develop a comparative advantage: the service sector, whether governmental or private services, or services to businesses or to households. A strategy moving in this direction may hold the most hope, but we need to know more about the composition of central city labor forces and about the employment and multiplier effects of the service sector.

2) Just as the nature of production in cities is changing, the role of some cities is shifting. Where once the cities were production centers, they are moving toward becoming consumption centers, particularly with respect to educational, cultural, and other leisure activities. Although these consumption aspects of the city may now contribute significantly to the economic base of only a few select cities, the potential of this role should not be ignored in designing economic development strategies for any of the older cities.

3) It is not only the private sector that is in ill health; the public sector is too. By offering fiscal relief and also by encouraging state and local equalization of tax burdens, the federal government can help all cities become more attractive and at least reduce the already heavy odds against declining cities. Let us remember that without adequate police, fire, sanitation, health, and educational services, cities cannot effectively compete, not even for new service industries.

4) The problems of the central city are not just problems of inadequate physical and financial capital. As one of our embattled mayors recently said: "Solving the capital problems of Newark will not solve the social problems." Although the social problems

of the city are among the most intractable, knowing their importance in the equation of the declining city should warn us about putting our sole reliance on private investment incentives.

I have described HUD's new role in central city and urban policy and my own concerns lest that role be tied too narrowly to economic development. The final point I want to make is that the quality of the policy rests inevitably on the quality of research. Too often policy moves along without the guidance of adequate research; sometimes we can only grope in the dark. Other times, in our rush to solve problems, we seem to ignore what we have already learned.

Because the demand for knowledge outpaces the supply, especially with respect to economic and social policy, sometimes the policy is put in place before we can evaluate its merits. Since this is unavoidable, it means the policy itself becomes the laboratory; so we build into our own programs, such as the action grants, monitoring and evaluation procedures to facilitate learning by trial and, perhaps, error.

Federal policy currently centers around locationally targeted economic development. Therefore, among our immediate research concerns are local employment and income multipliers for different types of activities, in particular in the service sector. We are also concerned with the way the location of economic activity can be influenced by policy. (A question that must also be answered is the extent to which the location of activity *should* be influenced, lest we be engaged in beggar-thy-neighbor strategies.) The research of Sandra Kanter from the University of Massachusetts, Boston, Bennett Harrison of MIT, and Roger Schmenner of the Harvard Business School has helped us to clarify the nature of location decisions by firms and their sensitivity—or insensitivity, as their results seem to suggest—to local tax incentives. All the same, we do not know whether tax incentives at the federal level would be more effective.

In addition to the research to help us evaluate and shape immediate policies, we need to encourage more long-term research on the nature of the city in the context of national and even international economic growth. The city is an open economy, and concentrating too narrowly on the problems within it will make us miss the more long-term forces which influence it, in particular continuing changes in the nature of production and its impact on income distribution, both functional and personal. The economic condition of cities and urban areas is the manifestation of these basic economic facts.

Since we are highly dependent on good research, additional new roles for HUD, the urban agency, are as patron and patron saint of urban research. (There are, by the way, some five saints named "Urban;" can this be an omen?) We are in the process of developing a public finance and economic development research group to shape a research agenda to be implemented both in-house and out-of-house. We hope to stimulate the production of that research by sponsoring not only individual contracts and grants, as we have done in the past, but also journal symposia and conferences. Our goal is to promote not just the production of research but its refinement, a refinement that results from cross-fertilization, a refinement that leads to new policies.

Jane Jacobs wrote about the economies that take place when you put lots of people with lots of good ideas together in the same place. What we at HUD are interested in is a city of scholars—whether the city is defined spatially in its usual sense or, as in a vision of the future, through the proximity of ideas.

The Federal and State Role

PART TWO

Federal Tax Policy and Urban Development

CHAPTER FIVE

George E. Peterson*

My subject is the Federal Tax Code and its impact on central city development, especially the development of older central cities. Perhaps I should begin by distinguishing tax policy from the other policies relevant to central city economics. First of all, the effects of the tax code on urban development are almost entirely inadvertent. Tax laws, up to now at least, have not been drafted with urban impacts in mind. One of the clearest examples of this is the history of the development of the tax advantages for owner-occupied housing. The essential tax advantage that homeowners enjoy is that they have an asset—their house—and according to the tax laws they do not have to pay income taxes on the economic benefits they enjoy from that asset as long as they occupy the house themselves. But they are allowed to deduct from their taxable income mortgage interest costs and property taxes just as if the house were an ordinary economic asset and one that generated taxable income. This way of taxing owner-occupied housing is very different from what is done in most European countries and Canada. The point I want to make at the outset has to do with the historical origins of this particular tax break as illustrative of what goes on in the tax code. It first came up in the emergency financing of the Civil War. It was proposed by Abraham Lincoln's administration as the way to treat housing income. That was a two-year emergency act, but ever since then we have simply

*George E. Peterson is Director of Public Finance, The Urban Institute.

copied the same language and maintained it intact. It was repro-
duced when the income tax was revived at the beginning of this
century, and it remains in effect today.

One hundred fifteen years ago it was nothing more than an
accounting convention, and it was not very important at that
time. But it is quite interesting to note what has happened since.
During World War II the income tax structure was greatly
increased to finance the war, and the average marginal tax rates
that taxpayers were paying jumped from about 4 percent to
around 25 percent. This suddenly made it of very practical significance whether one owned his own house and qualified for these
tax advantages or rented a house and did not benefit from that
structure of tax laws. There have been many rationalizations after
the fact as to why owner-occupied housing should be subsidized
by the tax laws. But the truth is—and this is just an illustration of
what generally goes on in the tax code—that our present system
was created by repeating without scrutiny language that dates
back more than a century, keeping it unchanged and even unexam-
ined, through a tremendous increase in average tax rates, so that
suddenly this long-standing legal distinction took on economic
significance and skewed the way markets operated.

The urban impacts of tax policy, then, need first of all to be
distinguished from the deliberate creation of urban policy. Second,
tax policy often has a distinctly secondary or even marginal effect
on urban areas and on urban development. This marks a distinction from the private market forces that underlie the central cities'
difficulties. Thus, the clout of federal tax laws should not be
oversold. They almost always work through private markets by
tilting cost and profit comparisons, by making the after-tax
ranking of investment opportunities different from free market
rankings of those same investment choices. But in most urban
markets they are of secondary importance as auxiliary to private
market trends. Nonetheless, at this point the federal tax code is
probably the closest approximation the country has to a national
development policy. As we move toward the articulation of more
explicit national growth objectives, it is going to be important to
keep in mind the effects that federal tax laws have in shaping
urban development, to examine whether these tax effects are consistent with what is going on in the rest of the deliberately created
urban policy. The administration's tax reform package unfortu-

nately presents a bit of irony in this context since, despite its substantial impacts for urban development, it was designed in almost all of its details before the official urban development policy was worked out.

In examining the federal tax laws, perhaps four lines of major influence could be emphasized by which the tax code does alter patterns of urban growth. The first comes under the heading of tax treatment of new construction versus tax treatment of repair and maintenance expenditures for preserving or upgrading older capital. Historically, the federal tax laws have greatly favored investment in new structures across-the-board over investment in repair and maintenance for the preservation of older capital stock. The effect of subsidizing new investment has been to shorten the useful life of older capital. That process is perhaps easiest to see in the case of machinery, where the explicit purpose of the investment tax credit is to subsidize the cost of buying new machinery for industrial firms and to squeeze out a lot of the older machinery that is still in use. When public policy subsidizes the cost of something like a machine or a piece of equipment it speeds up the replacement cycle and accelerates the scrappage rate. This does not have any particular locational implications—machinery is pretty much substitutable between all locations. But when tax incentives are used to subsidize the cost of constructing new buildings and are imposed upon urban development markets of the kind this nation has faced over the last 30 years at least, the effect is to accelerate the adjustment to other kinds of economic incentives. The bulk of old buildings in this country is located in the central cities, so with a subsidy for replacement of capital, the life of that productive capital is artificially shortened and its removal from the market is accelerated. Most of the new capital that is subsidized explicitly by the tax laws is being built in the suburbs and in the urban fringe of metropolitan areas or in the growing regions of the country, so that there is an imbalance in the effects of the tax laws.

However, it is important to make clear that the location of new construction is not ultimately determined by the tax laws, rather, for most locations, the fact that capital is placed in the suburbs or in the South and Southwest is a consequence of demographic, transportation, and other very basic trends in the post-World War II economy. What these tax laws do, however, is tend

to compress the period of adjustment. The tax incentives accelerate the replacement of capital and accelerate, therefore, the
locational changes that accompany this subsidized modernization
of the capital stock. So it is fair to say that old capital has been
scrapped at a faster rate because of the tax laws than it would have
been in their absence, and that, in effect, the bias of the tax laws
in favor of new construction has become a bias in favor of suburban and fringe development, or at least has accelerated that
development.

What are some of these tax differentials? For example, a newly
constructed rental apartment can be depreciated at a 200 percent
declining balance accelerated depreciation or some even more
attractive accelerated alternatives. Improvements to older rental
property, which has to compete with that new rental housing construction, however, are limited to depreciation on a 125 percent
declining balance schedule. So you have a differential between a
200 percent accelerated and 125 percent accelerated depreciation,
and the more rapid depreciation accorded new construction does
enhance the relative after-tax profitability of that new building.

Our tax laws do not recognize land as a depreciable asset.
Essentially they assume that land never changes its economic value
and that fact, in effect, provides a strong subsidy to areas where
land generally increases in value, which has been true in the last
three decades in the suburban fringe, and penalizes areas where
land is either constant in value or, as in many of our older central
cities, where it has been losing value for the last decade and a half.
So the fact that land is not considered a depreciable asset by the
tax laws introduces quite a distortion into after-tax profit comparisons. Another example affecting nonresidential property is
the change in tax laws in 1954 which was largely responsible for
the rapid rate at which suburban shopping centers sprang up in the
late 1950s and early 1960s. From having no differential, no
accelerated depreciation allowances at all, this change suddenly
introduced a 200 percent declining balance depreciation for new
commercial and industrial structures but maintained a straight-line
depreciation for older properties. This provided an important spur
to the suburbanization of those productive facilities, shopping
centers, industrial parks, in the 1950s and 1960s.

So far I have discussed the after-tax rates of return that
investors can gain. Looking at this from the other side of the

market, at the cost of borrowing capital, there has been a long tradition of using tax-exempt privileges to subsidize construction costs. Again, during the 1960s, tax-exempt industrial development bonds flourished. They are essentially devices by which public or quasi-public agencies borrow for the specific purpose of constructing pieces of industrial plant for private firms. Simply put, they are contrivances to let private firms borrow on the tax-exempt market. They were used during the 1960s, primarily in the South and Southwest, again to accelerate this regional and geographic transition in markets, to subsidize the cost of building new industrial plants for migrating firms. By 1968 more than $1.6 billion of this kind of investment was going on. In fact, competition between the states got so out of hand that the states realized that they were knocking each other out in having to grant such generous tax privileges even to maintain firms they already had. They finally petitioned Congress to curtail the practice so that they would not have to give in to temptation and continue this kind of quarreling over tax breaks.

In many of the more rapidly growing states it has become customary to permit private developers of major subdivisions, these very large blocks of subdivisions or industrial parks, to establish so-called municipal utility districts, which has a nice acronym of MUDs, and other special utility districts to borrow on the tax-exempt market. These are private firms, which are borrowing strictly on their own behalf, to build internal streets, schools, sewers, fire stations and so on. Florida has a law of this sort called the Community Development Act. It seems that the intent of this legislation is to encourage large-scale developers, the kind that were responsible for most of the growth in the 1970s in Florida, who are going to locate outside of built-up metropolitan areas. The law requires them to install all of their own capital infrastructure, from fire stations and fire trucks to sidewalks, and it has a requirement that anything else that may be invented over the next 20 years to better fight fires will also have to be paid for by the developer. But the point is that all this capital infrastructure, and it runs to several million dollars for the typical development, has to be paid for by the industrial developer. The local communities and the states refuse to do any of this borrowing on the public market, but they in turn authorize these private developers to establish development districts on their own authority and to use tax-exempt moneys to carry out this construction. So, in effect, you have considerable subsidization of development at the fringe of the metropolitan areas with local and state people saying that they do not want to pay the cost of the capital duplication but that they will pass this forward to the federal government and allow the developers to qualify for federal tax exemption. The general point I am making is that on the borrowing side as well, on the cost of capital, there has been an inclination to use tax-exempt moneys. A lot of these particular programs have contributed to an acceleration of capital development in the public or quasi-public sector in fringe areas. These too have been competitive with old central cities.

Now, let me be as clear as I can about what the tax laws do and do not do. First of all, they do not alter the incentives for the final location of a plant, or what the economists call the ultimate equilibrium outcome of the distribution of investment, rather, they compress this period of adjustment into a much shorter time frame. My own feeling is that the best way to view the current problems in urban adjustment is not in terms of the direction of movement or the fact that there is migration of firms and people but in terms of the speed at which this process is taking place. This is the problem with which we cannot cope. It is regional migration at a speed that leaves behind large pockets of unemployed persons, that thrusts the fiscal problems of rapid urban shrinkage on local governments, and that has led to great per capita cost increases and tax burdens. It is the speed of the process which we are not able to handle, and the federal tax structure has contributed to this compression of the time frame and acceleration of the adjustment process.

Secondly, what is done with the tax laws closely reflects what is done elsewhere. Parallel biases infect all of the federal attitude toward capital investment, as can be seen in the grant system as well as in the tax system. A general tendency exists to favor the construction of new capital over the preservation and retention of older facilities. Historically, the government has been very generous in subsidizing new interceptor sewer systems and in considerable part these systems have been responsible for suburbanization in particular metropolitan areas. The infrastructure is built in the outskirts. This lowers the cost of new development and that new development competes directly with the older facilities. Of course it is clear that this has happened with the highway system and highway subsidies. In the last year or two lawmakers have been working to change this aspect of the federal grant system. A new attitude toward federal subsidization of water pollution control is being developed which would restrict grants to replacement of what is weak in existing systems and prohibit their use for construction of new sewer networks in undeveloped areas. Similarly with the highways: the 1976 amendments to the highway trust fund laws for the first time explicitly spell out that repair and replacement are satisfactory applications of the highway trust funds. Again, the government is trying to shift some of the grants from new investment, new capital construction, toward replacement investment.

I want to point out an irony here in what is happening with the tax code itself. While the development of older central cities and with it the older capital stock that is their primary competitive advantage is being encouraged by some federal policies, there have also been versions of the tax reform proposals which would increase the investment tax credit from 10 to 13 percent and would apply it for the first time to industrial structures. The impact of applying from today or tomorrow a 13 percent investment tax credit for industrial structures would immediately open a tremendous gap in the after-tax cost of new construction, new capital, as against older capital facilities. This is exactly what theorists are trying to counterbalance in all the rest of the urban policies. The urban development action grants, the housing block grants, EDA's initiatives, are all trying to generate employment and generate investment in the central cities, and these are rather modest efforts. At the same time, there is a proposal for possibly $1.4 or $1.5 billion annually in newly created tax incentives to encourage the decentralization and more rapid replacement of industrial structures. This is the kind of problem lawmakers have to be on the alert for. One thing is being done with direct policies but is undone more powerfully with indirect ones.

The second theme I wanted to mention was the housing market and what the government does with homeowner subsidies. The biggest subsidy for housing in dollar terms is the tax subsidy. The way the Treasury calculates it, approximately $11 or $12 billion a year in tax expenditures, tax subsidies, goes toward owner-occupied housing. If imputed rent is included, as economists suggest, the figure goes up to about $25 billion per year in tax subsidies. The linkage with urban development is that a subsidy for homeownership historically, and it remains true today, has been a subsidy for a particular kind of housing—the low-density, single-family house. In the literal sense, in that it occupies its own lot, this has led to low density, but much more importantly it accounts for almost all the scatter of the development at the urban fringes, the kind of leapfrog development that, again, has made the fringe economically attractive and competitive with the older central cities. In fact, a study completed by The Urban Institute estimated that each one percent change in the relative cost of homeownership and renting in the tax system introduced about a half percent gain in the single-family share of the total housing stock. On average there is about a 15 or 16 percent artificially tax-induced favoritism for single-family housing which would mean roughly somewhere on the order of an 8 or 9 percent larger share of single-family housing in the total housing mix than without the tax laws.

Again, this is the kind of policy that runs parallel with many others: the Federal Housing Administration grants, of course, have run in the same direction. But what is peculiar about the use of the tax structure in this case is that it is very highly skewed to the upper income groups. Because tax deductions are used as the method of delivering the incentive, it is highly skewed to those in the upper income brackets where those deductions have the most value. The trends since World War II in housing ownership and in single-family housing construction are very interesting. While from 1900 to 1950 there was a gradual decline in the rate of homeownership in this country, from about 50 percent to a low of 40 percent, between 1940 and 1950 there was a jump from roughly 42 percent up to around 57 or 58 percent, and then a further jump to 62 or 63 percent in 1960. That may not sound so large, going from 40 percent to 60 percent in a decade and a half, but in comparison with the rate at which most social changes occur, it is a very, very rapid change. Examining the breakdown of that change we see that homeownership rates did not increase in the lower income brackets, where there are few beneficiaries of FHA insurance and other subsidies. There are very modest increases in homeownership rates at the low and lower-middle income brackets. The great jump occurs in the upper income brackets, and the timing coincides exactly with the effect of the World War II jump in income tax rates and the tremendous gap in after-tax benefits that occurred because of the increase in the marginal rate structure.

Based on the study by The Urban Institute, it seems clear that the federal tax laws have been responsible for roughly half of the net increase in homeownership during that 15-year period and that they were responsible for a great part of the increase homeownership in the upper tail of the income distribution.

Another piece of confirming evidence which I think very interestingly supports the same conclusion is a comparison of United States housing markets with Canadian housing markets. Canada's economic conditions are similar in many ways to those in the United States, but Canada does not allow mortgage interest deductions on income taxes, and it does not allow property tax reductions on income declarations. In Canada there is a much more even distribution of homeownership rates across income brackets. Upper income families are only 5 or 6 percent more likely to own their own houses than are the lowest income families. The United States trend cuts right across the middle of Canada's: low and lower-middle income brackets have much lower rates of homeownership, while at the high income brackets there are substantially higher rates of homeownership in the United States, coinciding exactly with the incentives built into the tax system and with the kind of shift in the United States structure that happened between 1940 and 1950 or 1955.

Between 1940 and 1950 there was a great increase in home-ownership rates in all kinds of structures. Then in the next decade, with about a five-year lag behind the tax law changes, this housing starts to phase out in favor of newly constructed single-family housing. Thus, historically the tax laws had a large effect in influencing development patterns in the 1950s and 1960s. They are much less important today in stimulating single-family construction for a variety of reasons, the primary one of which is that without much fanfare we have had a steady narrowing of the tax advantages of owner occupancy through the increase in the standard deduction. What happens is that as the tax laws are rewritten so that more and more people take the standard deduction and fewer and fewer people claim itemized deductions in their tax returns, the net advantage of being able to itemize mortgage interest and property taxes declines. Between 1974 and 1975, for example, we had 4 million fewer people taking the homeowner's deduction; 1977 will be down again with about 2 or 3 million persons including homeowner property tax and mortgage interest deductions as itemized expenses on their tax forms. So, on the one hand, we have had a somewhat narrowing of the tax advantages for the single-family housing. But again this policy includes a very great irony, in that for all our social rationale for subsidizing homeownership—that it is necessary to social mobility, it is necessary for neighborhood effects to encourage low- and moderate-income people to keep up their housing—by this increased generosity in the standard deduction, these people no longer even itemize. The estimates are that next year most people even in the $24,000-$26,000-a-year bracket will find it attractive to claim the standard deduction. This is the direction in which the tax laws are designed to go, and so the benefits of tax deductions are restricted more and more to the upper tail of the income distribution. Instead of subsidizing homeownership as a tenure form, we are subsidizing, in effect, larger and more expensive houses for more affluent members of the population.

Another important question is how the tax code is used to provide capital to the housing sector generally versus capital to the other sectors of the economy. In the United States tax incentives are one of the chief instruments for allocating capital among competing sectors of the economy. Given the relative stability in the supply of capital, how after-tax rates of return are allocated to different sectors has a large influence on the amount of investment that takes place, say, in industry versus housing, or in the public sector versus housing. I want to make two or three points briefly. One is it is clear that in the last decade of shifts, we have been moving quite steadily and in balance strongly away from the relative subsidization of housing. Housing has traditionally enjoyed a very large tax advantage in this country. But more recently, as we have become more generous with the investment tax credit and with a lot of the other measures designed specifically to generate industrial construction, the relative sectoral balance has been tipped quite a lot, and there are proposals for tipping it still further, diminishing the relative advantage that the housing sector has had. It is more a housing issue, I suppose, than a central city issue, but in fact the amount of investment that goes on in the housing sector probably has the largest of the tax impacts upon the shaping of urban development patterns. Housing has been the lead decentralizing force in the United States, the lead force in suburbanization. As we pour more money into housing, we are building new housing and upgrading housing standards at the expense of—or at least with the effect of encouraging the diffusion of—metropolitan economic activity. It is to the detriment of the central city that our policy encourages abandonment of housing and discourages the upgrading and maintenance of existing housing stock.

Let me illustrate that sectoral tradeoff in terms of the last public policy statement on housing goals—the 1968 Housing Act. That act called for construction of 26.5 million standard quality housing units over the decade between 1969 and 1978. If that act had been carried out, if those objectives had been secured, it would have required a vast redirection of national investment goals toward the housing sector. One study has estimated that even a pared-down version of that act, one that did not create as many deliberate vacancies as the law had called for, would have required a 75 percent increase in housing's share of gross national product, a 75 percent increase in a couple of years and persisting over at least a decade, going from about 3.5 percent of full employment GNP to over 6 percent. This would have meant very, very large changes in the sectoral allocation of capital and even more, of course, as a fraction of actual GNP rather than full employment GNP. The act called for building 25 million new houses and 26 million new and repaired units and scrapping 12 million older housing units. Thus it is clear that as new capital is poured into the housing sector the replacement of older capital accelerates. This policy called for the deliberate creation of 12 million vacated or abandoned housing units over the period of a decade, and those housing units were almost all located in the older metropolitan areas and in the central portions of those regions. Of course, no one would encourage that policy today, but there is always this tension between rates of new construction and the redevelopment of existing housing stock. The law called for the deliberate creation of 3.5 million vacant units, standing vacant units, just to depress rental rates in the cities. What is to be learned here is that that much capital cannot be redirected unless there are the tax laws to sustain it, and if the tax laws are adopted it is

imperative to be aware of these very large intrametropolitan implications because the suburban market competes directly with the
center city housing market.

The last point I want to raise very briefly is the direction in
view of all of this, that we take with the tax code. The foremost
conclusion I would urge is that we try to render that tax code as
neutral as possible whenever we can. If there is to be a major tax
reform, it ought to be moving in the direction of tax neutrality
wherever possible. This policy fits the objective of simplicity of
administration, and it certainly would have, in my judgment, a
favorable effect upon central city development.

Whether we should go beyond the establishment or re-
establishment of neutrality to try to introduce differential tax
advantages for the central cities is another issue. The Urbank proposal, for example, would increase the industrial revenue bond
authorization for central cities. There are proposals to have a
differential investment tax credit of 5 percent for investment
carried out in the central city. There was, under the Ford administration, and it probably will be revived, a proposal to have a
differential employment tax credit for central cities. These, in
my estimation, are much more difficult questions, but if we are
subsidizing central city investment through interest rate subsidies,
through subsidies of land assembly, through EDA policies, HUD
policies, or Urbank policies, at least we should aim for making
the tax code consistent in reinforcing those objectives.

EDA's Urban Economic Development Initiatives

CHAPTER SIX

Victor A. Hausner*

One of the great opportunities of upward mobility is that one can get further and further away from the problems and at the same time be given more responsibilities to deal with them. In this way one might interpret my career as having left New York just on the verge of discovering there was a serious problem. At that time, although New York City was making some interesting efforts, I do not think we in New York City or anywhere else fully appreciated the situation. We were still writing briefing papers trying to explain to Bell Telephone why they ought not to go to northern New Jersey and why they ought to stay in downtown Manhattan. I think we did not appreciate the seriousness of the problem.

That brings us to what might be one major point that I would like to bring today from Washington. Donna Shalala has indicated that we might expect a more realistic, lower keyed response to urban problems from this Administration. Although it will be clothed in some of the rhetoric that we all became familiar with in the 1960s, about urban needs and poverty and despair, a more realistic response probably will be formulated by an administration which is concerned with balancing a number of competing and conflicting concerns and which recognizes that it does not have the luxury of either excessive federal spending or the luxury of concentrating on single problems. This more realistic, low-

*Victor A. Hausner is Deputy Assistant Secretary for Economic Development Planning, Economic Development Administration, U.S. Department of Commerce.

keyed approach is to my mind one of the most ambitious initiatives in domestic policy, and one of the hardest tasks for any federal government to pull off.

As we launch into a period of increased public intervention in a deliberate, rather than an inadvertent way, to attempt to impact private sector investment, it is essential to proceed with great caution. I think in some sense it may well be a semirevolutionary step in domestic policy, the full consequences and the difficulties of which may not be fully appreciated in Washington. So, I am not sure that just because we might be a little more low keyed and a little more realistic, we are being any less adventuresome than other administrations have been with regard to domestic policy.

The blessings of long-term research and analysis are clear, but, unfortunately, at this point in an administration anxiously attempting to put its programs together, they are also a luxury. At the moment we are very much pressed at EDA, and we have been trying to rethink very quickly the directions that economic development policy ought to take and to turn those directions into programmatic options for the administration. It does not give a lot of opportunity for carefully reasoned effort, but then again I wonder if that is ever what occurs in government. Maybe one does a lot of warm up in the minor leagues and then grapefruit games for a number of years and then simply gets thrown into the game. We pray we are right in the biases and everything else that is accumulated over the years, because that is exactly how policy is developed. Maybe it is not such an unfortunate situation. In fact, we are getting an opportunity to find out whether some of our thoughts are valid.

We are faced with a lot of very, very difficult questions to which we really do not have solid responses. Many of the questions have impacts on diverse policies that EDA and other federal agencies are dealing with in various ways. Shifts in local, state, and regional economic bases have caused problems of attendant economic disparities. It is not fully clear how the interrelationship of those various economic bases is affected, or where the sources of some of the disparities actually lie, or what is the impact of the shifts in economic bases on certain target populations and on opportunities for these target populations. We are not clear about the impacts of international trade changes on the profitability of particular industries. The problem is not only spatial or geographic in character, nor is it only a question of target populations. There is also a question of the productivity of particular industries. Not a great deal of work has been done on the industrial sectors of the economy and how sectoral analysis might help us in some of the spatially oriented programs that we are trying to direct. There are questions of the differential impacts of trade, energy, and environmental factors on profitable enterprise as well. The government is now trying to respond to the steel situation. What is a capable, well-reasoned, and realistic response to the steel problem? To what degree are we watching the phasing out of obsolescent facilities and the introduction of new facilities in other regions of the country, while some areas are simply paying the price? There are geographic disparities in the resolution of industrial investment decisions.

Resource scarcities and shifting balances of trade between regions are problem areas. All the studies have indicated that areas with substantial agricultural production and energy production are improving their positions in trade relations with other regions of the country. Other problem areas involve capital markets and the provision of investment capital to small- and medium-size businesses: the question of whether there are or are not capital gaps and to what degree there are responsibilities on the public side to attempt to fill those gaps, the question of incubator industries in cities and the degree to which federal investment in those areas is an important element to economic development, the question of capital investment in obsolescent infrastructure of diverse industries. What about the mapping of the industrial facilities of this country to take a look at the differential distribution of obsolescence across the country? What are the ramifications of that for economic development policies?

Another set of questions can be formulated around technological change and regional economic disparities. An interesting book by Jeffrey Williamson and a colleague on the historical analysis of regional economic disparities from 1830 to 1950 is coming out. It is fascinating to put some of our present questions into that historical context. The critical role that technological improvements have played in regional economic disparities is clear. It was interesting to learn that in fact major technological changes in society and major regional economic disparities took place substantially between 1830 and the beginning of the Civil War, while the period we describe often as a period of rapid industrialization, the post-Civil War period to the beginning of the Twentieth century, was in fact a period of increased equalization between regions, because most of the technological changes had already seriously impacted the distribution of opportunity in the society.

All of this brings me to another point. I often find that much of the discussion on these issues—and this is not an unusual failing for American social science—is distinctly ahistorical in quality. It is as if we were born yesterday and had never heard of economic disparities and differentials in economic opportunity, that no economic modernization process had occurred in this country, and that we could not learn anything from the historical patterns both in this country and in other Western industrial societies that would provide us with important insights. Simply moving over into the international economic development field might give us some insights into alternative development strategy and some important questions as to who pays the price for adjustment. These are some critical questions, but the tendency very often is to see this, as we did right through the 1960s, as the urban crisis, to put it in ahistorical terms and therefore weaken our ability to assess what is occurring in the society. It is not new for the United States to use public intervention to impact private investment. I think Alexander Hamilton had that in mind when he funded the debt. I think that is what we were talking about with the provision of land to railroads. That is what we were doing with our canal systems. The idea that the society has just now come upon the notion of public intervention for economic development often surprises me. It is surprising that we find this such a violation of the traditions of the society when, in fact, the society has been built on it. The question may become more problematic when the decision is on intervention for whom, and not intervention. We have known for a very long time that we have a mixed economy. It is not surprising that George Peterson found that there are built-in patterns in the distribution of benefits in the tax structure.

On the subject of national economic policy, I think that there is a potential for emphasis on subnational, microeconomic questions—sectoral, spatial, and by population groups—to be the major initiative of the Carter administration in domestic policy. I do think that there will be recognition of the hills and valleys of our economy, of the various economic disparities, and not just attention to aggregate well-being. There will be a little more attention now to questions of subnational disparities, for both equity and efficiency reasons. There will be concern with a variety of problems for which subnational or microeconomic responses will be sought. There is a collection of adjustment problems—so-called problems of natural events, public policies, market forces—suddenly impacting the economic well-being of particular places and people, for example, the steel situation; major plant closures—the famous Studebaker closing in South Bend is a classic case for EDA; the natural diaster—Xenia, Ohio, for example; the shoe industry; the serious attempts by this administration to balance its commitments to free trade with its need to deal with the geographic ramifications of altering trade conditions. EDA itself has been dealing with shoes and steel, and with drought and energy impact: the impacts on community development and local economies of rapid growth in energy production in the western states and in Appalachian communities. There are areas in Kentucky where trucks go barreling down highways that cannot possibly tolerate for very long the weight of those mammoth coal-bearing transportation vehicles. What is the federal responsibility for aiding such areas, especially when long-term economic development planning seems less of an issue when the area seems to be booming? The possibilities of boom/bust cycles in oil shale development and in coal development in Appalachia are very serious problems. Here we have the whole issue of fragmentation of political power in the society between local and state and federal governments, and how it complicates dealing with those areas and people who are the recipients of the negative consequences but are not the beneficiaries of the profits and the revenues that are produced.

Next is the issue for which EDA was originally established: the chronic unemployment and underemployment in our society. Initially this was seen as the major issue in rural poverty; now it is increasingly seen as an issue for urban development. Then there is cyclical distress. Recently the EDA obligated $4 billion in three months. We funded 8,568 individual public works projects between July and September 30. It is an exhausting process and does not give one much time to assess the impact of all that investment. But the cyclical questions remain: cyclical distress, what is its incidence in terms of geographic distribution, how might we better prepare to deal with such distress in the future?

I would suggest, then, that we need targeted investment programs using diverse development tools—with a high degree of specificity and with a great deal of finesse in using the instruments—and that to deal with a diverse collection of structural economic problems is not a low-keyed initiative but rather a highly ambitious one. There are problems with such an initiative. As Julius Shishkin suggested, a major dichotomy is that federal programs are far outstripping the data that exist to administer any of them. EDA runs its program largely on the basis of one indicator, on somewhat faulty information which is two years old and which has to be rebenchmarked the year after we use it. With this kind of data resource we intend to run a highly targeted program of economic development. That is a problem for all of us.

Another problem involves the utility of particular development tools that we use. With all our tools—direct business financing of loans, loan guarantee programs, lease guarantee programs, public works investment programs, revolving loan programs—we do not have a good sense at this time of the utility and effectiveness of these tools. Hopefully, in the process of building evaluation programs we can learn a little about what we are accomplishing with the tools that we use. That has not been the case in the past.

There are really several levels of national policy with regard to these economic disparities that I have mentioned. One of them is tax policies. We have on the one hand a limited group of public development policies, community development, economic development, manpower development, and other such programs that have as their objectives some attempt to affect development between areas and between population groups and on the other the $460 billion budget, which can wash away the impacts of all of those targeted investments. And so, one level is the general impact of federal policies; tax policies, procurement policies, public works programs. In reading the special analyses that come out with the federal budget every year, I have always been struck with the fact that there is no serious discussion in them of the capital budget of the federal government. There is one interesting chapter which studies federal assistance to state and local governments and which indicates that the balance of assistance by the federal government between regions has slowly shifted to become more equitable between the Northeast and Midwest and the Far West, as the types of investments by the federal government have changed from hard-dollar public improvement investments in the West to social welfare expenditures in the Northeast and Midwest.

Well, it seems to me that it is about time we dug a little more deeply into that area to study the nature of public expenditures, not just the distribution and whether or not we are all getting a dollar back on a dollar given, but what is the nature, the form in which we get those returns. What are the ramifications of those expenditures on economic opportunities in particular areas. Very little work has been done there. The Congress has asked the Department of Commerce to do a major study over the next 18 months on the historical impacts of public works investments in the United States over the last 30 years. This is an extremely interesting subject. However, I am a little afraid that some of the questions we have asked far outstrip the available data, and it is going to be very difficult to make longitudinal analyses of these questions.

Another level of public policy is general development. Here we have the impacts of other functional development programs; environmental protection programs, transportation programs, housing and physical amenity programs. Those are community development programs, and we should know what the ramifications of those programs are on economic activity in different areas.

The last area is one I call economic development, and for the moment I will describe it as limited to public intervention to affect directly private investment for private sector job creation. We have found this definition useful at EDA to make some distinctions among various public policies. It seemed to us that some very important distinctions had to be made if we were to deal with economic development policy in a relevant way: to distinguish, for example, investment in sewers by EPA and investment in sewers by EDA. I suggest that there are differencces, and at those points presumably we have some other objectives in mind than those of the Environmental Protection Administration.

The coordination of these various levels of concern must be an important component of national public policy. How we are going to tie together the urban impacts of overall federal expenditures, the impacts of other types of development programs, and finally direct public intervention for job creation is an extremely complex task for this administration. Comprehensive urban economic development, which directly concerns EDA, in fact means addressing a number of problems. Some of the current discussion in Washington tends to focus around limited objectives, objectives not limited to economic development as a whole but limited within economic development. There is some tendency to look to new financing tools, a new institution, some new gimmickry, which will have appeal, which will seem like a significant response by the federal government but which may not necessarily be addressing the diverse problems we have. In fact we have diverse issues before us. Some of them relate to incentives for expansion and location of creditworthy businesses, firms that would be good to keep, to expand, or to locate in particular areas. Then there is the question of front-end investment to make areas more attractive for private investment and to facilitate new roles for uban economies. We may have to do serious front-end capital investment without an immediate private investor prepared to dive into an urban area. Such actions will involve a great degree of risk for the federal government, but the simple fact is we must either take a substantial amount of risk in our attempts to achieve economic development or we are going to play it extremely conservatively and look only for cases in which there are major opportunities. I would suggest that if the opportunities for private-sector investment were so great we would not be facing an urban economic development problem, and if we are too cautious in our wish to avoid the problems of urban renewal we might err on the other side and only choose to finance projects that most likely would have occurred anyway.

Another area for attention is the area of capital needs of small- and medium-size businesses that function less effectively in the credit markets. I am not talking about refinancing our own bad loans or about shaky firms that are going bankrupt. I am talking about firms that are profitable but do not give as high a return on investment and therefore seriously hinder economic development in central cities.

Still another concern is the question of jobs and incomes for target populations. Simply directing programs to improving the tax base of central cities does not give any assurance that the benefits will rebound to those chronically unemployed and underemployed in central cities. This is illustrated by a conversation I had with a past mayor of Oakland. He was discussing port development in Oakland, one of the major EDA investments in the past, and pointed out to me that Oakland was long considered one of the great economic development successes by some people of EDA. The mayor asked why this development was considered a success when three out of every five jobs, and more recently, four out of every five jobs in the Port of Oakland go to suburbanites. On top of that, to get the development, the City of Oakland had to forego certain tax returns from the project. The mayor put the very reasonable question to me: if we are not getting the revenues and we are not getting the jobs, in what sense is this an economic development success? As this example points out, it is not at all clear that an economic development program deals necessarily with economic disparities between population groups. It can be a program of "gentrification." We may in fact be engaged in a mobile poverty program in economic development. There is a possibility that we will rediscover the economic benefits of investments in central cities and help our poor to move to other places where they will still be excess baggage. So we have some serious questions about whether or not society will really address its poverty problems through economic development efforts.

Let me just touch on one last problem. In the discussion about mounting a nation effort for economic development, one of the key items in our thinking at EDA is: do state and local governments have the capacity to plan for and implement policies? Even if we provide a variety of sources of assistance to state and local governments for such economic development efforts, it is not clear that these governments have the capacity to analyze their economic situations, to develop investment strategies, and to implement them. I know that only too well from sitting in New York, trying to get deck chairs for the passengers while there was a mammoth hole from an iceberg in the hull. What we at EDA feel is needed are consistent streams of public investment to capitalize long-term investment strategies. No individual isolated projects, or new flashy institutions, or new development tools that we do not have in our kit bags now, are going to add up to a comprehensive federal urban economic development program. Unless we are prepared to put our dollars behind some meaningful assessments of local economic situations and to finance them over time, we will not meet many successes in our economic development efforts.

The objectives are multiple. We have to be honest with ourselves also. We are not talking about a massive attempt by the federal government to throw money to the wind. There is a margin for public action to achieve a variety of objectives. In some cases the goal is to mitigate the consequences of decline, and I do not think we should shy away from saying that. In other cases it is to reach an equilibrium level of economic activity which would have been lower if we had not intervened. For example, good things are happening in Detroit: the private sector is getting more involved, the public sector is building institutional capacity, there is great interest, the mayor of Detroit has friends in Washington and that will assist the city, Detroit has a better sense of its needs, better economic development programs will be mounted, and significant impacts may result—yet at the same time, some of the population of Detroit is going to move out.

We may find that what we call the urban crisis in the short to medium term may well be, in the long term, an adjustment to new economic roles. Possibilities of future growth understood in longer terms exist for some communities. For other communities there is managed growth which might involve retention strategies, expansion strategies, and new location strategies but have diverse objectives.

Now what about the EDA program. Well, in examining the program, it was decided that our kit bag was filled with tools—it wasn't filled with money, but it was filled with tools. We also found, in an assessment of EDA's own investment patterns in the past, that there was a serious inadequacy in terms of piecemeal projects and uncoordinated investments and a lack of the critical massing of our resources. Of course this is not wholly a problem of EDA's own investment strategies. It is a difficulty faced by any agency living under the aegis of the Congress without presidential support, indeed with presidential ideological opposition to the notion of intervention in the private economy. Finally, we found that despite the agency's main involvement in rural development, EDA has made and is making investments of some $500 million targeted in urban areas. I would suggest that some of the most innovative efforts in urban economic development anywhere in the country are those being funded by EDA and that the reality is that the federal government has not financed a great deal of direct economic development investment.

The EDA program that we are proposing, therefore, argues for an alteration in the way we think about what we do. One aspect is an increased emphasis on capacity building. Using our planning and technical assistance programs, the agency wants seriously to strengthen the capacities of state, metropolitan, and local governments and neighborhood development institutions to plan for and carry out economic development programs and to develop long-term investment strategies into which EDA can place its resources in multiyear investments. In reading overall economic development plans (OEDPs) it is clear that we could usefully pay some attention to modifying those plans so that the agency actually got investment strategies that included priorities, time frames, assessments of economic opportunities—areas of concern that do not appear in OEDPs today. We have a start toward this with our 302 program. This program is now providing comprehensive economic planning and policymaking assistance to 40 major central cities in the country and to 47 states. The 302 program emphasizes direct involvement by the private sector in the process of policy making and planning for economic development and an intergovernmental framework. We hope that with 302 assistance at the state, city, and neighborhood levels, and at the metropolitan level as well, policy makers can then be moved to develop some sort of vertically integrated process of federal planning and development implementation, through which not only EDA but the entire federal development assistance program might be able to function, financing locally developed investment strategies in some coordinated fashion.

A second aspect of our program is an investment program which coordinates EDA's various development tools in customized responses to local structural economic problems by financing long-term investment strategies. We feel we have the flexibility and latitude at EDA to mix and match our tools as appropriate and to put the major emphasis on long-term investment strategies at the local level.

Third, our adjustment program recognizes that along with chronic economic distress may come a variety of sudden economic impacts that can have substantial effects on a community, either by launching or by accelerating chronic economic problems. While the tools might be the same, the responses to short-term distress and to longer term distress may differ in particular ways.

Fourth, we plan a research and information program which recognizes that we will not be able to conduct this kind of economic development program and that state and local governments will not be able to plan and implement their programs if they do not have the relevant information on regional and state and local economic trends and if they do not have a sufficient understanding of the utility of different economic development tools. My strong feeling is that EDA's research programs have produced some very valuable information but that we have paid a minimum of attention to the effective dissemination of that information so that it can be actively and effectively used by development practitioners and economic development planners.

Finally, we are offering for consideration by the administration, a standby, countercyclical, public works assistance program which we hope will allow for a federal response closer in time to the trough of a recession than the present federal record of between 29 and 42 months after the trough. So while EDA might be heroic in its obligation of $4 billion in three months, unfortunately the trough of the recession was back in 1974, so we were a little late.

Thus, we have broken up the EDA proposal into four programs, recognizing that there are different economic problems that ought to be addressed at different spatial levels. The proposal includes a city program which will be concerned with the tax base and with general strengthening of the economic base of the central city as well as job opportunities for central city residents. Since that alone may not be enough to respond to the particular problems of target populations and target places, there is also a neighborhood economic development program. Its particular focus is job intensive economic development, with a view to creating jobs that can directly benefit the chronically economically disadvantaged and the neighborhoods within which they live. Third is a metropolitan program under which we will try, on a demonstration basis, to address central city and urban problems within a labor market area context, knowing at the outset that it is going to take some effort to reach a multijurisdictional approach to economic development and not putting an enormous amount of our effort into what is probably the toughest aspect of this problem. Finally, there is a state program. We have an extraordinary opportunity to involve state governments, both in a regional context and at the substate area level, in greater support for urban economic development efforts and for assistance to target populations. With the support of other federal programs, we may be able to use our own state 302 planning assistance programs and our 304 state investment programs to provide a sufficient carrot to industrious states that are willing to enter the field to support urban economic development efforts.

Clearly, the issue of urban economic development is not the only issue of economic development in Washington. EDA chairs both the economic development subcommittee of the President's urban and regional policy group and the economic development subcommittee of the President's rural development policy group. While the economic analyses are different, the issues and the questions are very much the same. I would suggest to you that probably one of the most interesting aspects of this administration, and one of the areas in which we may have some of the most creative impacts, is in the area of subnational economic development: at the regional level, at state levels, and at multijurisdictional levels, both urban and rural. The question is do we have the courage to take up the cudgels on the issue of subnational economic development.

Urban Economic Adjustment Strategies: The State Role in Michigan

CHAPTER SEVEN

Waino H. Pihl*

It is no accident that my paper is titled an Urban Economic Adjustment Strategy rather than an Economic Development Strategy. Some declining central cities may never regain the metropolitan area dominance, population density, and economic vitality that they once enjoyed. We should encourage these urban areas to accept this situation and adjust to new functions; in fact, these new functions may offer a higher quality of life to those who remain in or are attracted to the central cities in the future. The higher quality may be manifested through higher regional service functions and lower population densities that are accompanied by less congestion and pollution.

In Michigan, we are beginning to think of the central cities' future as containing more quality and less aggregate growth in population, income, and economic activity.

My discussion of urban economic adjustment strategies will be divided into six sections: first, a description of the urban problem; second, an analysis of the forces causing the urban problem; third, potential solutions or components of the urban economic adjustment strategy; fourth, an assessment of the political and economic feasibility of potential solutions; fifth, the partnership responsibilities or roles of government and the private sector in defining and implementing adjustment strategies; finally, some components of the Michigan urban economic adjustment strategy.

*Waino H. Pihl is Director, Office of Michigan's Changing Economy, Michigan Department of Commerce.

Michigan's governor has a keen interest in urban economic adjustment strategies. He has encouraged Michigan's state and local governments and private institutions to work together to ease the plight of Michigan's central cities. At the 1976 Republican National Convention, the 1977 National Governor's Conference, and numerous other occasions, Governor Milliken sought to focus attention and policy development efforts on the urban problems of the nation. The governor and Detroit's Mayor Young are of different political parties but are actively working together to solve Detroit's economic and social problems.

Urban problems are not new, but they are worth restating because our perceptions dictate our problem-solving strategies. The central cities' acute social and economic problems manifest themselves through 1) depreciated and obsolete public infrastructure (e.g., sewer, water, public utility, and transportation systems); 2) vacant and almost obliterated residential dwellings, commercial strips, and industrial buildings; 3) concentrations of poor and unskilled who have the greatest need for, and the least ability to pay for public services; 4) the flight of businesses and middle- and upper-income families to the suburbs, essentially a migration of the tax base across political boundaries which separate these people and the tax base from the problems of the central cities; 5) high crime rates; and 6) structural unemployment.

This urban problem syndrome, when combined with burgeoning fiscal difficulties, creates an almost insurmountable problem for a central city. The growing municipal service demands by a low-income population, combined with the geographical separation of the central cities from potential municipal revenue sources, severely aggravate the cities' fiscal problems. The increasing economic base of the suburbs that cannot be tapped by the central cities to serve their growing municipal needs frustrates many central city budget directors.

What forces precipitate the urban physical problem and resulting urban fiscal problem?

The precipitating forces are the natural maturation of a manufacturing-oriented economy, combined with government policies that generate artificially lower costs for locating in selected area. These artificial cost differentials have coincided with a changing employment mix which is a response to labor-saving technology and to changing consumer tastes. The combination is reflected in

1) the move from manufacturing employment toward service employment; 2) the filtering down of firms from the manufacturing cities of the Northeast and Midwest to low-wage areas of the Sunbelt region; 3) the movement of firms to the suburbs where there are inexpensive and large land parcels that can accommodate sprawling industrial and commercial facilities; and 4) the movement of industry toward high technology centers.

This change in employment mix and migration of firms away from the Midwest and Northeast or to the fringes of the central city erodes the city's economic base and leaves behind the immobile, poor, and low or unskilled people. Such people usually have the least ability to pay for, and the greatest demands for municipal services. They demand welfare, crime and fire prevention, transportation, health services, and education. Many of these services are supported largely by local revenues, although others receive significant support from state and federal sources.

Besides the fact that migration of employment leaves behind unskilled, poor, immobile people, migration also leaves behind depreciated or obsolete buildings and infrastructure which clutter the horizon and impede the development of new industry and new service employment. New businesses must expend significant sums of money to clear the land of vacant buildings. Central cities must maintain or upgrade public infrastructure that has depreciated or become obsolete in order to attract new businesses.

Urban physical problems which are most apparent in the mature, manufacturing-oriented northeastern and midwestern cities may also appear in the rapidly developing southern cities as they mature. As I said earlier, urban *fiscal* problems arise from political fragmentation and the tendency of people and industry to move away from the problems of the central cities. These problems are not limited to northeastern or midwestern cities. They may arise in southern or western cities that cannot expand their boundaries as the tax base migrates outward from the central cities.

What are the characteristics of potential solutions to urban physical and fiscal problems?

Urban problems are by nature long term, carrying over many political administrations and legislative sessions. Any real solutions must also be long term and require significant cooperation and sharing of resources. Most of all, they require difficult and crucial decisions. Their implementation requires significant public and private support, analogous to religious fervor, aimed at redirecting or revitalizing central cities.

Public and private decision makers must first define the future function of central cities and, second, develop and implement policies to realize that future function. These future central city functions might include at least the following alternatives: 1) a revitalized and restored city that dominates the metropolitan area and serves as a hub of economic activity; 2) an urban reservation for the immobile, poor, and unskilled: or 3) a specialized economic activity node in a multinodal metropolitan area no longer dominated by the central city. This central city may offer a higher quality of life and better municipal services than it did in the past.

The future function of the central city depends on the relative feasibility of implementing the following four strategies: 1) revitalizing the central city while discouraging suburban sprawl; 2) directing the immobile, poor, and unskilled toward areas of greater economic opportunity outside the central city; 3) implementing cutback management programs for central cities; 4) continuing to promote economic growth at the fringes of central cities and sharing this suburban tax base growth with the central cities.

Once the decisions are made, a variety of policy levers exists to implement these adjustment strategies. Michigan is in the process of making many of these decisions and identifying the appropriate policy levers.

What is the nature of a politically and economically feasible economic adjustment strategy?

To begin to reverse or decelerate the economic trends of the central cities, suburban politicians must be convinced that suburban economic and social vitality may significantly depend on the central city's economic and social vitality. These politicians must also acknowledge that the central city's revitalization or redirection may slow suburban population and economic growth but that this slower suburban growth may not be harmful. Many suburbs lose their luster as they become congested or begin to overload the capacity of their municipal services; this is particularly evident in the inner ring of suburbs. Some of the dividends from new suburban development, particularly industrial and commercial development, may have to be reinvested in the central cities to maintain the metropolitan area and suburbs as attractive places to live.

This interdependence argument often is not acceptable to suburbs because they may view themselves as relatively independent of the urban core city. Suburbanites frequently move to the suburbs to avoid central city fiscal responsibilities. Even if the interdependence argument is accepted, the degree of suburban economic support to core cities may not be sufficient to reverse the trends.

If central cities continue to decline, many older suburbs near these cities may also follow in the wake of the core city. In Michigan, suburbs and small cities (25,000-50,000 population) which are on the far outer fringes of the central cities are currently experiencing growth due to business and residential migration from the core cities. These communities, if they are well interconnected by transportation routes, may hold the metropolitan area's future. These cities with large economic growth potential must speculate on whether they can survive without the central city. Their decisions may significantly influence the fate of the core cities. If the central city decline is just beginning and these fringe cities have not realized much growth, they probably do not envision much potential growth, and view their role as supporting the central city rather than growing independent from it.

Other arguments for suburban political and economic support range from conserving scarce resources (energy, land, and central city infrastructure investments) to just plain Christian charity for the poor and unskilled residents of the central cities.

If suburban political and economic support for metropolitan or state government initiatives cannot be sufficiently secured, then a relatively larger share of the economic aid must come from the federal government.

Once the political feasibility has been initially assessed, the economic feasibility must be reviewed by answering at least three crucial questions. 1) How much do the cost differentials, which currently favor suburban business and residential locations, have to be revised to encourage movement back to the cities or a cessation of out-migration? 2) Will this migration deceleration occur through natural forces as cities depopulate and more open space is available in the central cities? 3) Are there unique qualities of central cities that will attract businesses and residents when cost differentials, low crime rates, and high quality municipal services again favor central city locations?

The spending requirements for reversing cost differentials, reducing crime rates, and improving municipal services are not known. Together in an urban partnership, local, state, and federal governments and the private sector may be forced to experiment with adjustment strategies and programs before accurate cost estimates are available. In fact, such experiments may provide the information necessary to answer the economic feasibility questions. Action must be taken while central cities still have sufficient resources to help themselves move toward their future functions.

To focus Michigan state government efforts on developing an urban economic adjustment strategy, Governor Milliken established the Urban Action Group consisting of key state department heads, including Commerce, Management and Budget, Labor, and Social Services. Our Department of Commerce director, Dick Helmbrecht, was named urban policy coordinator for this group. The Urban Action Group organized a series of roundtables on urban fiscal and social issues, including housing, crime, neighborhoods, youth employment and education, and economic development in order to identify problems and develop solutions. These roundtable discussions included local, state, and federal government and private-sector participants. The Urban Action Group is nearing the completion of the series of conferences. Upon completion, an Urban Economic Adjustment Strategy will be developed and suggested to the governor.

The Office of Michigan's Changing Economy, of which I am director, provides technical and economic research support to the Urban Action Group. Even though our research and policy development efforts are more oriented toward a statewide economic adjustment strategy, we realize the importance of Michigan's central cities.

Recently, my activities have been very urban oriented. I have been reviewing with the City of Detroit's budget and planning people how the state can assist Detroit with it *fiscal* and *physical* urban problems. The following discussion of potential urban partnerships will summarize some of our conclusions.

As was discussed earlier, an urban economic adjustment can be oriented toward at least three potential functions for the central city: an economic activity hub for the metropolitan area; an urban reservation for the immobile, poor, and unskilled; and a specialized economic activity node in a multinodal metropolitan area.

To move toward at least two of the three potential functions, significant cooperation and resource sharing among state, local, and federal governments and the private sector is necessary.

The federal government's partnership role can include establishing a stable national economic climate that will benefit cyclically sensitive central cities and neutralizing, where possible, cost differentials that encourage *interstate* and *intrametropolitan* migration patterns. These cost differentials arise from the location of federal installations; federal aid formulas; R and D funds; grants for economic development; assistance programs for transportation, water and sewer, and housing; and tax and financing concessions for business and residential housing.

Local governments must learn to live within their economic means while providing social services in a cost-effective fashion; this includes cutting back on services when there is a decline in demand, or willingly shedding services that can be more effectively provided by the private sector or at a higher level of government which draws on revenue sources that better match the service market area.

Local, federal, and state governments cannot facilitate economic adjustment of central cities without cooperation from the private sector, whose movement away from central cities has largely been a response to government sector signals. The private sector needs the proper signals, including tax incentives and high quality public services, to remain in or move to central cities and to make the long-term private investment that can move central cities to a new and brighter future.

State governments can play an important role in the economic adjustment of central cities. City governments obtain their taxing and spending powers from the state government. Also, state government can provide economic assistance to central cities using a variety of ways which can be ranked in a hierarchy of indirect to very direct participation. Beginning with indirect participation, the state can do the following. 1) Pass enabling legislation that permits local governments to offer tax exemptions for business on local taxes. The city determines which businesses receive these incentives, and the city bears the direct financial costs. In this case, the city's role is also somewhat indirect; it does not make direct investments but encourages the private sector to do so. 2) Provide technical assistance to cities through state-enabling legislation. Control of the incentive and its financing still remain in the hands of local governments, and the decision to invest is left with the private sector. 3) Offer tax credits on state taxes to the private sector for employment or investment made in central cities. The state administers and finances the program, while investment decisions are left to the private sector. 4) Establish umbrella organizations to coordinate state and local economic development activities that induce private sector investment and employment. 5) Support central city municipal services financially and leave the administration of these services with the local government. 6) Provide directly some of the municipal services that are largely consumed in central cities but also are consumed statewide (for example, zoos, cultural and recreational activities). 7) Invest directly in central cities through the placement of state facilities and by developing or maintaining public infrastructure. 8) Regulate site locations of public and private facilities such as electric plants, sewer line extensions, highways, and hospitals. 9) Regulate financial institution lending areas in order to prevent red-lining in urban areas. 10) Establish local government taxing and spending districts.

Initially, Michigan offered indirect support to the central cities, largely in the form of enabling legislation, but now the state is moving toward more direct involvement.

The state government role can also be defined in terms of the jurisdictional limits of federal and city governments. State governments provide city governments with taxation and spending powers and authority to offer tax inducements to businesses. Thus, although the federal government may target its tax exemptions or spending on central cities, it cannot directly authorize changes in local taxation or spending. Federal grants or revenue sharing, however, can finance the construction and maintenance of infrastructure that permits local tax reductions.

The state government can broaden taxing and spending districts, thus diminishing their proliferation. Once these districts exist, the federal government can nurture them through targeted subsidies, such as grants, tax exemptions, or low-cost financing, that encourage economic development in selected areas.

Central city governments are responsible for effectively managing their fiscal affairs and encouraging economic development, using powers and resources provided by the state combined with resources provided by the federal government. Central city economic development is constrained by limited powers and resources which are particularly crucial once the economic base begins to erode. At this point, state and federal governments must provide more administrative flexibility and more resources. The federal government should be viewed as the primary source of resources; it has a significantly larger resource base than state governments. It also has the ability to influence business location patterns throughout the country as well as patterns within a metropolitan area.

In Michigan, many groups, including the governor's staff, the legislature's staff, and the Detroit Economic Growth Council, have been investigating solutions to the plight of Michigan cities. The recommendations cover five major areas.

Assessing the feasibility of sharing of industrial tax base growth in the southeastern Michigan area. Currently, we are formulating a tax base sharing system that will share tax base growth among southeastern Michigan municipal governments according to their needs and ability to pay for local services.

Revitalizing central cities through: 1) establishment of downtown development authorities and economic development corporations which facilitate the acquisition of land for industrial and commercial development by the use of tax exempt financing, condemnation, tax incremental financing, and local property tax exemptions; 2) establishment of property tax abatement programs to encourage business investment; 3) establishment of a job development authority that will lend low cost capital to existing businesses; 4) proposed new business development corporation that will provide equity and debt capital to new ventures; 5) proposed employment tax credits to employers who hire employees in the central cities; 6) proposed training programs for unskilled employees working in central cities.

Easing the fiscal burdens of central cities by providing financial assistance for high quality public service and for services that are used throughout a metropolitan area or statewide. Michigan has established a $28 million state equity package to assist Detroit's cultural and recreational facilities, to reduce unfunded pension liabilities for Detroit's Department of Transportation, and to place state police patrols on Detroit's expressways. Besides the equity package, the state has established a $12 million urban grant to cities levying income taxes.

Studying modifications of existing state enabling legislation that encourages local economic development, modifications which will provide the necessary flexibility and operational funding to make these programs effective tools.

Assessing the feasibility of helping central cities to operate land banks that assemble large, fully developed land parcels suitable for significant industrial development.

In addition to revitalization efforts, Michigan is studying policies that will discourage urban sprawl by providing the proper market signals to the private sector. These signals will indicate the real cost of using scarce land and energy instead of the current signals that encourage low-density housing and business patterns.

Michigan's urban economic adjustment strategy is oriented toward a public and private sector partnership and is emphasizing feasible solutions to urban problems that will mobilize resources at all levels of government and the private sector.

In addition to the governor's Urban Action Group, the City of Detroit, the State of Michigan, and the private sector are implementing an umbrella organization for Detroit economic development activities, including public and private activities. The organization will coordinate these activities in the central city sector of Detroit. Another recent noteworthy effort to revitalize Detroit includes the construction of the Renaissance Center, financed by a consortium of major Detroit employers.

The decision to revitalize and redirect the central city are part of a conscious effort to preserve valuable resources present in large infrastructure investments already in place; cultural and social functions performed by the city not supplanted by the suburbs; the 25 percent of Michigan's population that lives in the central cities; and the industrial base existing in the central cities that offers potential input sources or final markets for the products of firms located anywhere in the metropolitan area.

I hope that I have not led you to believe that the Michigan state government is trying to usurp the functions of local government. It is not. Local government has always been closest to the people, and because of that it will never be replaced. The role of central cities in their own revitalization cannot be understated. Local governments are clearly the most important participants. Nevertheless, they cannot go it alone. They need help from the federal government. The federal government will continue to be the principal supplier of economic resources.

Between local and federal governments there is a broad role for state governments. They must provide enabling legislation that will permit the flexibility to devise new economic development and technical assistance programs. State governments must also provide direct investments as well as incentives for private investment that will reduce and more realistically align the location cost differentials between central cities and suburbs.

Michigan has rejected the notions that central cities should become nothing more than urban reservations for the poor or that they can regain the metropolitan area dominance that they once enjoyed. Michigan views the central cities' future somewhere in between these two extremes—as a specialized node in a multinodal metropolitan area. I have tried to outline the policies Michigan may employ to permit central cities to serve this function.

Revitalizing Central Cities: More on the Myth of Sisyphus

CHAPTER EIGHT

Richard Gordon Hatcher*

Shortly before he died, the sardonic British writer Somerset Maugham addressed a college level class in creative writing. During the question-and-answer session following his remarks, Maugham was asked by a dewy-eyed freshman, actually, a freshperson, about the secrets of novel writing. The author of *The Razor's Edge* looked the questioner in the eye and said: "There are three classical rules for producing literature of the highest order. Unfortunately, nobody knows what they are." To paraphrase Maugham, there are several basic rules for revitalizing cities and for reversing the urban decline of the post-World War II period. Unfortunately nobody has had the vision, the moxie, the will, or the political longevity to translate these rules into consistent, long-range national policy.

When I first took office as Mayor of Gary in 1968, much seminal work—head work, legislative work, work shaping public opinion—had already been done on behalf of urban America. Important urban initiatives were under way—initiatives that could have made a difference in the state, and status, of our urban areas. With the will of Sisyphus, and the help of administrators like Joseph Califano and Robert Weaver, President Lyndon Johnson had pushed the urban boulder close to the summit of Mount America. And then came Chicago and the Democratic convention of 1968, and the election of President Nixon. Today, a half gener-

*Richard Gordon Hatcher is Mayor of the City of Gary, Indiana.

ation later, eight years after the end of the Johnson era, we are back at the bottom of the hill, dusting ourselves off, shoulders to the boulder, pushing back toward the summit of Mount America once again.

With more optimism than I have had in many years, I would like to make several modest proposals on methods for revitalizing central cities. I shall limit myself to three basic themes. First, to help preserve urban America, we must begin working to end racism and its effects; second, we must provide cities with the tools and tangible resources needed to offset the lure of the suburbs; third, we must end the national war against the leaders of urban and minority constituencies.

I must make it clear that in my judgment the urban problem in America today is inextricably linked to racial discrimination in this country. Thus, if we are serious about ending urban decline, we must come to grips with the legacy and the reality of American race discrimination. As Dr. Chinitz has pointed out in his funding proposal submitted to the Economic Development Administration: "A recent monograph by the Institute for Research on Poverty at the University of Wisconsin concludes that racial discrimination in the labor market and deficiencies in human capital are far more important than housing segregation in explaining the low earnings of inner city minority populations."

Black Americans and brown Americans, by and large, have not yet had a chance to review and comment upon the monograph. But let me tell you something: the next time the lights go out in Harlem, in Bed-Stuy, and in the South Bronx, I want you all to remember that the resident sociologists on 125th Street and Lexington Avenue are familiar with the conclusions, and the significance of the conclusions, of the research team in Madison. And this familiarity breeds violence and despair, as well as contempt.

Affirmative action programs are among the best measures we have designed to date for reversing the effects of our unequal, and inequitable, history. But, at this moment, affirmative action programs are under a broad and bitter attack throughout the country. The Bakke case is just one front in a national campaign to continue rolling back gains toward racial equity made in the sixties. The implications of the Bakke case extend far beyond the academy, far beyond the question of finding fair and equitable standards for medical school admission.

The Bakke case has a bearing upon cities and their future. Inner city residents face a profound and growing shortage of basic medical services and medical care. From a municipal administrative perspective, this means that the City of Gary must spend one-sixth of its 1977 community development allocation—about $1 million—to underwrite development of a medical center complex. Alan Bakke, whatever the merits of his case, whatever his grade-point average at the University of Minnesota, would be a most unlikely candidate for establishing an inner-city medical practice. The 16 special admission students at the University of California's Davis Medical School are more likely to make their services available upon graduation to inner city residents.

Now is the time for all men and women committed to a better future for the cities of this country to step forward and shape the national debate over affirmative action. The counter concept of "reverse discrimination" has been given far more currency than it deserves. Congress recently passed a multibillion dollar public works bill. Some 10 percent of the funds were to be set aside for minority contractors. Last week, the California Supreme Court agreed with a national contractors' association that this special allocation was unconstitutional. Thus, the public works initiatives in Los Angeles and elsewhere have come to an abrupt stop.

The attack upon targeting funds and opportunities to the neediest people, and communities, in this country is gaining momentum. From 1968 through 1976, there was no need for anti-city and antiminority leaders in America to mobilize their forces and to redirect public opinion. Our national political leaders and the Congress were committed to sharing the national wealth with the rich as well as the poor. The "New Federalism" expressed in the revenue sharing and community development block grant programs provided feasts for affluent communities and famine for fiscally ill cities and their residents.

The times have changed. The new national administration is considering pinpointing federal dollar allocations and opportunities more carefully. The new community development regulations will call for targeting three of every four dollars to areas of need.

I believe there is a new willingness on the part of our national leaders to attack poverty head on. I also believe, however, that a strong counterreaction is underway. Leaders of the counter-attack can draw upon the distaste for active presidencies devel-

oped within the past few years. Groups opposed to disturbing the
status quo—groups opposed to demolishing institutional racism
and structural barriers to urban development—can also draw upon
the poisoned public atmosphere that is the chief legacy of previous
national leaders. The social programs of the sixties were dis-
credited by the Watergate warriors. It will be extremely difficult
to erase phrases like, "You can't throw money at problems," from
the national consciousness. The counterattack against affirmative
action and against minority group advancement draws power from
waters that run fast and deep. For that reason, I believe the policy
shapers committed to building better cities in a better America
must begin speaking out. Without vocal and visible support from
such organizations as the Center for Social Analysis, it will be
extremely difficult to build a new national consensus on helping
poor people and distressed cities. And without strong public
support for urban programs, and for programs to redistribute
opportunities in this country, the national administration will have
difficulty in finding the will to act.

The second theme I want to address involves the provision of
basic tools to city administrators and the provision of economic
incentives for the development of urban areas.

City governments are entering the economic development
game rather late in the day. Although most sizable municipalities
now have economic development agencies, few municipalities have
the funds needed to hire, train, and retain professional economic
development administrators. Over the past ten years, local governments have focused in large part upon building physical development capacity and upon providing survival services for dependent
local residents. I think it is fair to say that local government has
taken its cue from agencies on the federal level. Up to the present,
the focus of bureaucracies like HUD has been on physical development efforts, on promoting construction of housing and neighborhood facilities.

Suddenly, agency heads and administrators are beginning to
take another look at the way cities work—at the types of things
they do and don't do. A basic redefinition of roles is under way.
Urban economic development is now in vogue. Unfortunately,
cities across the country are floundering because they have little
experience in initiating and conducting economic development
activities.

The National League of Cities at its most recent annual meeting adopted a resolution calling for a national program to provide economic development help for cities. Specifically, the resolution asked for federal dollars to underwrite economic policy planning and planning and analysis. I supported this initiative. I also supported the prospective increased involvement of EDA in central city development. Central cities will have to catch up if they are going to stem the flight of businesses to suburban shopping malls. Unfortunately, core cities are not able to afford the game without a sizable infusion of federal assistance.

Cities also need greater access to capital to assist in offsetting discrimination by financial institutions in the private sector. When banks refuse to lend funds to inner-city homeowners and entrepreneurs, cities must be given the tools to step in and provide essential support. When insurance companies retreat from commitments to inner city clients, while federal and state agencies stand idly by, cities must be given the tools to provide the security demanded by homeowners and merchants. When private sector developers turn investment dollars into suburban shopping centers and apartment complexes, cities must be given the wherewithal to launch new capital projects in central cities.

In Gary, we are struggling to reconstruct our downtown business district. The initial support for this effort is coming from the public sector. Our task would be infinitely easier if an urban domestic development bank were available. As it is, we must tap every available city and county agency for support and assistance. As we concentrate our limited dollars downtown, we shortchange our neighborhoods, we postpone repairing streets and sidewalks in other business districts, and we pile up problems for the future.

The Carter administration is developing a tax reform package. The President's economic advisers are looking for a tax code that is based upon the three pillars of equity, simplicity, and capital formation. As we all recognize, equity can mean many things to many people. It is important that equity for cities—equity is permitting cities to compete more effectively with suburban jurisdictions—be one outcome of the tax revisions. Currently, capital investment incentives conspire to undermine central city development and rehabilitation. The economic lures cities need, and can receive, through tax code revisions, include 1) investment tax credits for accelerated depreciation on equipment and facilities located in areas with high unemployment rates; 2) tax credits for job creation in high unemployment areas; and 3) tax credits to encourage inner-city landlords to undertake substantial rehabilitation of existing buildings.

The provisions of the tax code that favor homeownership and discourage rentals must be removed. The tax advantages and shelters that make it more profitable to build new shopping centers than to rebuild downtowns must be revised.

For decades, central cities have been laboring under enormous developmental handicaps. Downtown America did not simply collapse of its own weight, or fall due to malfeasance, misadministration, or natural demographic changes. The centers of our center cities were tried, sentenced, and punished for crimes associated with race, class, and age. The time for the rehabilitation process to begin is long overdue.

The final point I wish to make concerns what used to be called pogroms. We are currently in the midst of a new surge in black political advancement. Oakland, California recently elected its first black mayor. New Orleans has also opened its chief executive's office to a black man for the first time. These gentlemen inherited troubled cities, and I am sure the congratulations they received were mixed with condolences from people who know something about the state of our cities today.

But there is another element widely acknowledged in Black America, yet hardly recognized in White America, that should give the friends of these new officials cause for concern. It has been clear to me for some time that black political leadership in this country is under attack. The targets of the attack generally do not address this issue in public forums. I have chosen to make this point for several reasons: first, it seemed clear to me that this issue would be overlooked even though it has a real bearing upon the revitalization of central cities. Second, I believe that silence on this issue has helped prolong the pogrom and has given its instigators and agents an anonymity they find useful. Third, I do not think it is possible to talk about black advancement and urban renewal without talking about the attempts to blunt both by discrediting black leadership.

Recently, a group known as the National Association of Human Rights Workers released a study entitled, "The Dilemma of Black Politics." The subtitle was, "A Report on Harassment of

Black Elected Officials." The study contains an overview of the long-term effort to suppress black dissent in this country. It also contains numerous case histories, including some information on attempts to undermine my administration in Gary. The report is far from complete; some elected officials who have received special attention from the IRS, the FBI, and other intelligence agencies have obviously chosen to remain silent, rather than respond to questionnaires and calls from the authors of this document.

I think everyone should know that it is possible for a local administration to be driven into a state of near paralysis by a kind of police-state harassment. It is possible to divert energies and time needed for developmental efforts to other pursuits, including long conferences with lawyers about the intricacies of the Fifth Amendment. Rather than focusing on grand plans, too many black officials have been forced to focus on grand jury proceedings. The cities now under black administration will never reach their potential until the tapping, bugging, harassing, and discrediting are curbed—until the pogrom is ended.

I am almost tempted to suggest that HUD establish a special agency to protect black officials from the outrages of agents within the Department of Justice. Then housing work and economic development work can proceed with greater speed and unnecessary impediments.

Recently, Georgia State Senator Julian Bond was in Gary to participate in a high school academic contest. Julian is one of the few black leaders willing to talk often, and aloud, about the activities of "Big Brother." Julian told me a rather amusing story. About a year ago, as he was boarding a plane, a beefy airline security guard strolled over and said: "Mr. Bond. How are you these days? I'm a great follower of yours." Naturally, Julian was delighted and surmised that the admirer was angling for an autograph. "I'm flattered," Julian said, reaching for a pen. "No, you don't understand," the security guard said. "I used to follow you for the Army Intelligence Agency."

One day, the war against the cities, and the war against Black Americans, and the war against Black American leadership will be over. It will be sooner rather than later, if more people determine that they want a just America and then stand up and speak out.

The Local Role

PART THREE

Strategic Issues in Local Economic Development

CHAPTER NINE

Dale L. Hiestand*

The literature on urban economics and the economic development of cities has by now fallen into certain patterns. We know about the losses of manufacturing and other activities to the suburbs, the South, and the West and about the growth of the service sector. There is a regular litany of policies and programs to promote economic development: policies with respect to land assembly, zoning, clearing; aid for industrial financing and facilities; manpower, educational, and training programs and policies; transport and traffic policies with respect to highways, mass transit, airlines, railroads, and waterways; policies and programs with respect to local public services, amenities, environment, housing, and safety; cost policies, including taxes, power rates, other regulated costs, and wage rates; generalized promotional efforts; information and marketing; ombudsmen for business; and so on.

I would submit, however, that economists have not been particularly helpful to political leaders, public officials, or businessmen in formulating strategies for economic development. The primary reason seems to be that economists tend to look at problems in a different way than do political leaders, public officials, and businessmen. Economists, like other scientists, are trained to develop broad generalizations, usually on the basis of large scale data. Economists usually try to deduce what is common or average about certain classes of events or relationships. Inherently, their

*Dale L. Hiestand is Professor of Graduate School of Business and Senior Research Associate, Conservation of Human Resources, Columbia University.

analyses are based on the past, and they hesitate to forecast. Rather they feel more comfortable when they project or extrapolate past relationships.

In contrast to the economist and his generalizations, the businessman and the public official deal with the particular. The businessman may be interested in what happens to businesses in general or to businesses of a particular sort, but he makes decisions with respect to his particular business. Similarly, economic development at the local level is concerned with one central question: what policies and programs will work in *my particular* city?

The crucial point here is that each central city is in some measure unique. Each city has a significant number of relevant distinctions which must be taken into account. Theorists have recognized this by using classifications of cities in our economic analyses: Duncan distinguished manufacturing centers from service centers, and between national, regional, and subregional cities. Stanback distinguished among nodal, manufacturing, resort, governmental, medical/educational, and other cities, using up to nine size classifications. Others have distinguished cities by whether they were growing or declining, whether they were "old" or "new," and whether they are in the Sunbelt or the Snowbelt.

However useful these rubrics are for analysis, they are much too broad to be very useful in developing an economic development strategy for a particular city. To replace generalities, there has been a slowly developing movement toward the analysis of particular cities in a comparative context. Ben Chinitz's comparison of the economies of New York and Pittsburgh over a decade ago is a case in point.[1] A second case is the detailed comparison of Chicago and Detroit by Meyer, Kain, and Wohl in terms of the distribution of jobs, residences of whites and blacks, and the transportation systems of each city.[2] More recently, Ronald Abler and his associates working in the field of geography have objected to the notion that "a city is a city is a city." They put out last year *A Comparative Atlas of America's Great Cities: Twenty Metropolitan Regions.*[3] Their purpose was to identify the similarities and, more particularly, the differences in the 20 largest cities in order to help develop urban policies which are sensitive to these differences. Karl Taeuber, in analyzing changes in residential segregation, asserts: "There is no typical metropolitan area . . . there are prevailing patterns of racial population change, but the specific pattern in each metropolitan area takes on a unique size and shape."

The emphasis on particular situations in particular cities is clear in the studies of coordinated urban economic development by Victor Hausner and his associates at the National Council for Urban Economic Development. My own thinking was stimulated in a project Eli Ginzberg, I, and our colleagues did for the Rockefeller Brothers Fund, which led to *An Economic Development Agenda for New York City.* My ideas have further developed in a study which Dean Morse and I are completing entitled *Comparative Metropolitan Employment Complexes: New York, Chicago, Los Angeles, Houston, and Atlanta.*

Now, of course, it has always been clear that local problems require local solutions. But this truism hasn't been given the importance it requires either conceptually or in our analyses. The most important difference among cities is in their industrial structure, particularly but not exclusively in their export or economic base sectors, which are usually the focus of economic development efforts. To produce an economic development strategy for New York City requires a thorough understanding of at least five interdependent sectors: 1) the garment industry and its related markets, showrooms, suppliers, designers, transportation system; 2) the financial district and its legal, accounting, printing, and other service adjuncts; 3) the corporate headquarters and midtown complex of offices, advertising, communications, business services, hotels, restaurants, and entertainment; 4) the international sector, including multinational and foreign corporate offices and international finance, trade, travel; and 5) the local governmental and nonprofit sectors, which are heavily dependent on direct federal and state grants, loans, and contracts, and indirect money flows via welfare, Medicaid, Medicare.

Each city has a different set of key sectors. Chicago has its set of financial, trade, convention and related activities to serve its region and the nation, its heavy manufacturing, and its printing industry. Los Angeles is strongly dependent on aerospace manufacturing, research, and development. Houston's growth is primarily based on its port, petrochemicals, and its growing role as a center for capital, largely on the basis of the huge cash flows from oil and similar depletion allowances and profits.

It is not enough to identify the particular industrial sectors which underlie the growth or decline of a particular city. What is required is a fundamental understanding of the dynamics of each sector. Each sector is made up of a multitude of subsectors and individual firms, each with its own set of managers, professionals, and workers, and each with its own position in various markets, its unique set of capital equipment, its own suppliers, transportation possibilities, and so on. Unless and until those contributing to economic development policy understand the dynamics of each sector and of the broad range of firms within each sector, it is not possible to determine what policy instruments can make a difference in retarding the decline or accelerating the growth of that sector—that is, what differences in the viability of particular sectors, subsectors, industries, and firms can be brought about by changes in land availability and zoning, the availability of facilities, manpower and educational programs, transport and traffic control, public services, amenities, housing, safety, taxes, wage rates, power rates, other regulated costs, and still other economic development efforts.

Each significant sector and industry needs to be analyzed in terms of key factors affecting its changing cost structure, technology, and markets, as they affect the expansion, contraction, establishment, or relocation of the broad range of firms in the industry. More importantly, these have to be studied in terms of the changing competition between each city, on the one hand, and its suburbs, other cities, the rest of the country, and, indeed, the rest of the world, on the other. Finally, one needs to assess the range of levers which can be manipulated at the local level to change the terms of competition for activities, and the impact that the manipulation of these assorted levers can be expected to have on the attraction and retention of each business activity.

This is a large order, and obviously cannot all be done at once. But it points out the directions in which our interests, research, and analyses need to go, if economic science is to provide a cumulative body of information, theory, and advice relevant to the economic development of each central city.

Of course, underlying forces affecting the industrial structure of particular cities often determine their economic growth dynamics, essentially independent of analysis, policies, and programs. Houston's rapid growth is in large part due to the dynamics of agricultural, oil, and mineral activities in the Southwest, although its political structure and business leadership can also be credited for carefully nurturing the city and its interests. The fortunes of Los Angeles have been tied to climate, water, and Air Force contracts. These formerly helped the city and region grow; in recent years these factors have made for irregular and slow expansion. New York's leadership has been largely helpless to deal with the out-migration of light manufacturing and corporate headquarters. Similarly, New York's leaders have played little part in promoting the rapid expansion of its international sector since the early 1970s. Even the planning officers of international banking firms seriously—but happily—failed to anticipate the rate of growth of international activities in New York City.

Not only is each city to some extent distinctive in its industrial structure, each city is also distinctive in its geographical setting, in its land use configuration, and in the complex set of private and public investments which go to make up its industrial and office system, its residential system, its transportation systems for goods, people, and information, and other elements of its infrastructure.

New York City, for instance, is a very highly focused city, with a mass transportation system capable of assembling large work forces in Manhattan for huge office and manufacturing centers. Because New York is broken up by a complex system of waterways and islands, automobile and truck traffic is often highly congested not only in the central area but also at the various bridges and tunnels. New York's garment and other light manufacturing is housed in a quite aged system of loft structures; its system of office buildings is relatively new; and its system of highway and other infrastructure investments contains many parts which are clearly superannuated.

Chicago has a different structure, for its manufacturing, warehousing, and similar centers tend to lie some distance to the south and west of the business center. There is only limited interaction between these parts. The southern industrial areas of the city also tend to be residential and ethnic enclaves, while the downtown area interacts mainly with populations and work forces from the north and northwest. There is also a series of intermingled residential and business districts along the city's east-west axis as well as the airport and related motel, conference, and business services to the northwest. Chicago's capital structure seems to be intermediate in age and obsolescence, in somewhat better shape than New York's industrial, transportation, and infrastructure system, but not as new in terms of its stock of office space.

Los Angeles is the polar opposite of New York in many ways. Its highway system is a grid with little focus, and its industrial, office, warehouse, and other kinds of business centers are quite dispersed and are intermingled with its residential neighborhoods. Los Angeles does not have the capacity to bring huge numbers of workers into a center and therefore has a relatively small downtown agglomeration of financial, business, service, governmental, and related activities. By eastern standards, moreover, it has a relatively young stock of public and private capital and infrastructure, although water supply problems continue to limit the growth and spread of the local economy.

These are only general comments about three cities. But they suggest that each complex of industrial, residential, transportation, and related investments has to be analyzed in great detail in terms of its current and future usability and obsolescence. These analyses have to be related to the profitability and viability of the key industries in each city and also to the impact of these industries on resident industries and on the quality of life for all who live in or visit each city.

Each city is unique also with respect to its human resources system. Each city has its own particular complex of public, parochial, and private elementary and high schools, junior and senior colleges, universities, technical schools, and the like. Each city's industrial structure tends to determine its mix of internal promotion and training systems and the character of mobility between and within employment systems. Each city has its own unique set of manpower training programs, employment agencies, and placement offices.

It is an oft-repeated platitude that human resources investments make a difference in the economic viability and attractiveness of different cities. I still believe that platitude, but I want to suggest that we have not carefully thought it through. For example, New York City and Los Angeles both make an unusually large investment in education through a complex system of institutions; in contrast, Houston's educational program and institutions seem stunted. Yet Houston is growing rapidly, Los Angeles is growing slowly and irregularly, and New York City is declining. In- and out-migration of manpower in response to changing industrial and occupational growth patterns obviously plays a part. How local education systems and training programs may be used for local economic development in an open system of cities is a puzzle which remains to be carefully studied.

Economic development is much more political economy than it is economic science. This means that an economic development program has to be developed in the light of social, political, and institutional realities and possibilities. These too seem to differ significantly from city to city. In each city, business leaders tend to have a distinctive style in economic affairs, industrial relations, and political influence. Trade union power, structure, and style tend to vary among cities. The relative size of ethnic and racial groups and the quality and style of intergroup relations also varies greatly from city to city. Finally, each city tends to have a distinctive political structure and style.

In Chicago, for instance, mayors tend to be strong political executives. Chicago mayors tend to maintain effective relationships with both trade unions and business interests. The Chicago political system seems simultaneously to protect business and economic development interests, provide fairly efficient services, keep taxes low, and provide jobs in both the public and private sector via its patronage system. Ethnic interests are powerful; race relations are sometimes difficult; patronage and public service systems are carefully cultivated on a direct basis deep into both the white and black neighborhoods, even though there are frequent public conflicts with some black leaders.

New York is usually considered a liberal city. However, ethnic politics are very important, and blacks and Hispanics have little political power. The political structure is closely related to real estate, banking, construction, and trade union interests. However, New York City's business leaders tend to be more involved in national and international interests and are relatively uninfluential in city politics. Mayors are reasonably powerful but rarely seem to be leaders. So many powerful interests have virtual veto power over almost any initiative that mayors spend most of their time negotiating among the power groups, including powerful public employee unions. The politics of the city tend to be antibusiness; economic development is supported in the breach, but there seems to be no effective economic development constituency.

Los Angeles is in many ways more liberal than New York with respect to intergroup relations and the role of blacks and Hispanics. Business leaders in Los Angeles tend to strongly identify with the city itself; they have an effective Chamber of Commerce which is trying to build the Los Angeles downtown and regional economy. The political structure is relatively benign: the mayor has only limited influence, while powers often seem scattered among leading members of the City Council. Business interests tend to be somewhat conservative, attitudes toward trade unions are mixed, but there is widespread agreement on the need for federal contracts for the aerospace industry and for governmental action to deal with water supply and environmental problems.

Attention to the political structure and its relation to economic development is important for several reasons. Some groups benefit from economic development; others may not. Even among those who stand to benefit, there are often struggles over just how the gains of economic development are to be allocated via the market and the political structure. Among the contestants for these gains are local landowners and other real estate interests; local workers who may be employed in the new enterprises; the construction industry and its trade union membership; the local banking, utility, service, and retail structure; and the local government, which wants more taxes in order to make life more rewarding and pleasant for local officials, public employees, and the leaders of public employee unions. Besides all these claimants, enough of the income flows generated by any new expansion must remain with the new enterprises to make them rewarding and profitable to their managements and investors so that they will make investments in the first place.

However, important local interests often fear economic development. For some, economic development means increased congestion, pollution, and other changes which interfere with the local quality of life. Some employers fear new competition for workers and space, reflected in higher wages, land costs, and office rent rates. Many citizens fear demands for added services and higher taxes to serve new enterprises, their related activities, and added population. Some resist because new growth inevitably alters the local political and social structure, including an increased number of "outsiders."

Still others on the local scene tend to be indifferent to local economic development. Well-established local business, professional, and other interests may feel they have little at stake, one way or the other. Indeed, those employed in large parts of the local retail and service structure may see no connection between their welfare and local economic development. Economic development is not an issue which appeals to many older people or women.

Blacks, Hispanics, and some other central city residents may have little reason to support urban economic development if nearly all the rewards go to executives and others newly entering the city and to commuters from the suburbs. Many blacks, particularly, remember urban renewal as "black removal" and are suspicious of economic development.

The point is that the gains to be realized via economic development may have to be fairly widely distributed if the necessary degree of local support is to be marshalled to implement the necessary policies and programs. How can a city's leaders change the terms of the existing political balance in favor of economic development?

One example is provided by Atlanta, where successive mayoral administrations, white and black, have had to negotiate the changing positions of blacks and whites against a backdrop of a continuing potential for economic growth. When white administrations and business leaders were in control, they negotiated with the black middle class leadership for changes in political rights, public service programs, and employment opportunities for blacks in order to avoid protests that might scare off potential branch offices, warehouses, distribution centers, decentralized manufacturing operations, and so on. With a change to a black mayoral administration, blacks have tempered their power. They have limited their demands for greater services, equal rights via school busing, and even demands for better jobs in the private sector in order not to frighten off businesses which might relocate into or expand in the Atlanta area.

This suggests a further point. Economic development is only one of many policy issues in the local political scene and may or may not be congruent with other local political needs. For instance, the rising emphasis on neighborhood or community control and neighborhood economic development creates risks for overall economic development in New York City. In general, one can applaud efforts to promote, protect, and rebuild particular neighborhoods. However, neighborhood control may create vetoes over certain large projects which may spur the city economy but are considered unattractive or unpleasant by all neighborhoods in which they might be located. Examples are the proposed convention center and the westside arterial highway.

One must also be alert to the competition for municipal funds, for they represent jobs in the central city. Public employee unions, ghetto leaders, and others may look askance at economic development expenditures and tax reductions in the interests of economic development, if health and other services are to be cut back and members of their constituencies are to be unemployed.

The implication is clear. There can be no prepackaged set of economic development policies and programs, good for all or even for many central cities. In each city, a set of policies and programs has to emerge out of the realities of its industrial structure and opportunities, its existing set of public and private capital investments, its institutional patterns and possibilities, and its community and political structures and possibilities.

Economic development strategies may be industrially oriented, such as those which try to protect or enhance local garment industries, the aerospace industry, petrochemicals, the international sector, or any other sector which is promising or in trouble. On the other hand, the strategy may be focused on key elements which cut across a variety of industries and sectors, such as land assembly, zoning, or clearing; aid for industrial financing and facilities; manpower, educational, and training programs and policies; transport and traffic policies: rail, water, auto, truck, mass transit, and air; policies and programs with respect to local public services, amenities, environment, housing and safety; cost policies, including tax levels, power rates, regulated transport costs, and wage rates; the local "climate" in terms of the style and quality of political processes, business leadership and organization, antibusiness movements, industrial and trade union relations, and intergroup and racial relationships.

Other key elements of an economic development policy are intergovernmental, involving the search for federal or state facilities and contracts, policies to build up and protect each city's metropolitan area, region, or vital customers, and the active struggle for federal and state funds and the shift of costly responsibilities from the cities. Here, too, each city has its own unique set of problems and possiblities.

Each city, based on its own economic, political, and social realities, will have to devise organizations to help focus these activities. They may be primarily in the government, as in Chicago and New York City; primarily in business organizations, as in Los Angeles and Atlanta; in a mixed form involving both government and business, as in Houston; or in a complex government, business, and trade union effort, as in New York State.

Finally, the time horizon for economic development is crucial. Political leaders obviously have to worry about the next election. But the economic position of a city, that is, its advantages and disadvantages, elements in its local cost structures, the general climate with respect to business, and its political style, all change slowly. Trouble may gradually make itself evident over a decade or two; efforts to alter fundamental patterns may also take decades. The development of a local political economy which can promote desirable economic transformations and also respond to fortuitous setbacks and good fortune, requires careful, foresighted, painstaking leadership and attention to strategic factors by business, government, and all the other participants in the local arena.

REFERENCES

[1] Chinitz, Benjamin, ed., *City and Suburb: The Economics of Metropolitan Growth* (Englewood Cliffs: Prentice-Hall), 1964.

[2] Meyer, John R., Kain, John F., and Wohl, Martin, *The Urban Transportation Problem* (Cambridge: Harvard), 1965.

[3] Abler, Ronald Francis, ed., *A Comparative Atlas of America's Great Cities: Twenty Metropolitan Regions* (Washington: Association of American Geographers), 1976.

Community-Based Development in Urban Areas

CHAPTER TEN

Stephan Michelson*

Despite the many social, political, environmental, and economic complications, the key to development is capital placement. The question is how much capital to place, where, and in what form (factories vs. stores vs. open space vs. "human capital" vs. housing, or clean factories vs. dirty, etc.). Whether products are destined for a market or for direct use, development implies an increase in standard of living, and this happens through the placement of appropriate amounts of the appropriate type of capital, operated under appropriate control. Development is not growth, but, like growth, it requires attention to capital placement decisions.

Policy is the determination of what institutions are best suited to make which decisions, and how to choose, monitor, and influence those institutions. Policy determines what kinds of results are to be achieved and what actors are best suited to achieve them. Policy implementation requires choosing the actors and influencing their performance.

My task is to outline a proper role for community-based groups in a central city development policy. For this task we need a theory. From the definitions of development and policy, given above, the theory we are looking for has three elements 1) what capital placement would be best, in terms of certain categories which need to be defined within the theory, 2) what institutions are most capable of making decisions about the actual kind of

*Stephan Michelson is Director of Research, Center for Community Economic Development.

capital to be placed where, and what institutions are the most capable of getting it done, 3) understanding of organizational behavior, so that a system can be developed based on the ways the most capable institutions respond to incentives, structuring the incentives so these institutions produce the particular capital decisions which produce the desired results.

Even with a theory of capital placement, relevant institutions, and incentive structures guiding institutional behavior, we cannot have a development policy without an accounting system which allows us to specify what outcomes are desirable and to determine if they are occurring. A great deal of current research is an attempt to describe the response of certain institutions to certain incentives, in certain accounting terms. The institutions are almost always individuals or for-profit firms. The incentives are income and price variations. The accounting terms are dollars, weighted and counted according to market prices and quantities.

I will not present a new accounting system here. I will, however, show that the limitations on the current system, as well as the lack of a well-developed theory which would lead to a correct policy, have joined to impose the wrong mandates on community groups, asking them to do things which they would have no particular advantage in doing, in places where what they are asked to do probably cannot be done at all, and in the end judging them—under these incorrect terms—to be failures. I will present, if not a complete theory, at least a fundamental conceptualization of the kinds of capital placement activities one wants in a development policy, with an identification of the kinds of institutions best suited to determining which specific capital placements to make, once the activities are identified at the policy level.

Besides a theory of capital placement and an accounting system to measure it, it would be helpful to look at some previous efforts to democratize control of capital. Since that analysis should relate to the theory, the theory should come first. And so it will.

PERFECT MARKETS

The capital market is usually considered as close to a perfect market as one can find.[1] It does what markets are supposed to do:

buyers and sellers both think they are price takers, and there is a homogeneous good, money. Differences of opinion about the soundness of various uses of that money generate bids, which allocate capital resources. Successful uses of capital generate more opportunities, as losers are systematically weeded out. The market's criterion for "good decisions" is clear—a return to the capital sufficient to replace it and leave a surplus. Saying it is close to perfect is saying that it is able to make good decisions most of the time. Capital goes where it makes a high private return.

To interfere with the capital market requires at least one of two positions: The capital market is not perfect. Capital funds *do not* go where they make the highest return. Or, a perfect capital market does not allocate capital correctly. Capital funds *should not* go where they have the highest return.

Anyone willing to argue for a different capital placement procedure, which is what a development policy requires, must be willing to argue that some current capital placement decisions—either *where* capital goes or *what form* it takes—are wrong. Thus, capital decisions made under a development policy must at least be different from those made by capitalists, and they should by some criterion be better. They can be better only if current allocations are wrong. And the capital market can be wrong either because it fails to follow its own rules (and other institutions could do this better), or because its rules, when followed, do not maximize social welfare.

Let us start with the second proposition, that even well-made private capital decisions are somehow wrong. The argument is simple, in a sense elegant, and very important.

THE COSTS OF PRODUCTION

There are two kinds of costs of production: monetary and nonmonetary. These are by and large substitutable. Wastes are dumped into streams as nonmonetary costs, borne by people down stream (and sometimes monetized by them as they clean their water). Waste disposal is surely a cost of production, though, and when governments prohibit the nonmonetary disposal, either a firm pays to dispose of waste in some other manner or, because its real costs have been monetized and this makes its products too expensive, it goes out of business. Since nonmonetary costs are often monetized later, the definition should be applied at the point of production. The implication is that nonmonetary costs—those which are nonmonetary to the firm—become monetary costs to other people. The ability of the firm to escape from monetizing costs is its ability to distribute the cost of production to others.

Not even all monetary costs are paid by the firm, however, and not all nonmonetary costs are externalities in the sense that they affect people who have nothing to do with the production process. Costs can occur within the firm or outside it, in monetary or non-monetary form. A simple matrix presents the possibilities:

	Internal	External
Monetary		
Non-Monetary		

An example of a monetary cost external to Logan Airport in Boston, for example, is the insurance rates paid by residents of East Boston who live near a jet fuel pipeline. Whether that cost is paid by current residents or was capitalized into the price of land (reducing rents and land sale prices) can be debated. If it has been capitalized into the land, it was the former landowners who took a capital loss, uncompensated by the Massachusetts Port Authority, when the pipeline was built. If not, current residents pay high insurance costs. Either way, Logan has passed monetary costs on to others.

A more interesting monetary cost is that imposed on a population by the decision *not* to place capital there. This is particularly striking when the capital was there in the first place and relocation of the capital occurs with disinvestment in the original location. Labor is then forced to reduce its wage demands in competing for the remaining jobs (and competing for replacement capital) and is forced to move where capital is locating. Thus, rural-urban and east-west migration, all paid for by workers, have been dictated largely by capital placements. The monetary cost of labor relocation is not to the firm, and therefore, does not enter directly into the capital allocation decision. It is a cost imposed first on those who are left behind, and then on those who follow the capital.

Nonmonetary external costs have become a cause célèbre in recent times, though they have always been part of the production process. The nonmonetary external cost of living with airplane noise is well-known and has forced MassPort to ban the Concorde under the local option recently granted it. That means it will not impose more cost, not that it will discontinue the current costs. Nonmonetary costs internal to the firm are most vivid in industrial accidents. Accident prevention programs convert this to internal monetary cost, and industrial liability converts part of it to internal monetary cost. Recently, we have learned of production processes which sterilize workers. Earlier, we learned of processes which debilitated or killed them (such as black lung and asbesteosis). These are nonmonetary costs paid by people involved in the production process, hence internal to the firm.

Obviously, what the perfect capital market would be perfect at is making decisions based on only one of the four categories, internal monetary cost. Just as obviously, what communities often get upset about is external costs, both monetary and nonmonetary. To the extent that a community is also the workforce, then internal nonmonetary costs are also an issue, but one of the phenomena of the modern city is that the residential community and the firm's work force are seldom close enough to being the same people that one organization can worry about all the costs. Thus, unions and communities, despite some overlap, often see themselves as opposed. Both are trying to pressure the company to spend money, one on safety of workers, the other on reduction of external costs.

The conceptual difference between internal monetary cost and total cost creates the possibility that minimizing one does not minimize the other. One could, and should, go through the same kind of analysis for benefits. Given the conversion between monetary and nonmonetary—and to some extent between internal and external—costs and benefits, actions to minimize internal monetary cost or maximize internal benefit are unlikely to minimize total costs or maximize total benefits. Thus, for example, when a city sells off surplus or tax-claimed land to the highest bidder, it is asking for that use of land which externalizes and non-monetizes cost. It then finds that it needs rules to get thse costs within certain requirements—no dumping, noise restrictions, and so on. It soon finds that it is in competition with other cities who are willing to bear more external costs, and all cities end up in unpreferred, suboptimal situations.

The story is old and, one would think, well known. The community group which says it will internalize external costs into its decision-making process, is saying it will make decisions differently from the private capital market—different and better. The capital market has failed. The capital market is perfect, but that perfection brings about the wrong results. Since it will now bear additional costs of production, however, the group may be promising too much if it also says it will make a profit.

One more important point must be made about the limited view of cost which the capital market considers. Accounting systems have been devised as an aid to business, particularly as an aid to decision-making by managers of private capital. Since the only costs those managers care about are internal and monetary, these are the only costs which appear in standard accounting systems.[2] When a government development program adopts standard accounting procedures, it is biasing all decisions against those which would differ from private capital decisions. This is a major failing of the one development program with which I am most familiar, and will be discussed below. I suspect it is a failing of all development programs.

IMPERFECT MARKETS

Many community groups insist that there are profit-making opportunities within their areas, opportunities which are not grasped by those who control capital. Some have proved their point. Without question, the Community Development Corporation which has most successfully demonstrated opportunities missed by the private capital market is Kentucky Highlands Investment Corporation. Originally called "Job Start," it is located in poor counties in the Kentucky hills. A Community Action Agency in Knox County spun off a CDC in 1967 to create jobs. In 1968 a ten-county CDC was formed, and it was funded under the Special Impact Program of OEO (SIP) in 1969. Initial attempts to run wholly owned businesses, using only indigenous skills and materials, led to small, marginal companies making toys and furniture and raising pigs. When the strategy shifted to inducing entrepreneurs to develop the local skills, a tent manufacturer and a kayak manufacturer, with heavy equity investment from the CDC, moved in. Between them, they employ over 100 people, earn in the neighborhood of $100,000 a year in profits, have $2.5 million in assets, well over $1 million in annual sales, and generate the secondary economic activity all that implies.[3]

Other cases are less clear. Two successful supermarkets in Denver, owned by the CDC, were taken over when large chains moved out but before the private capital market had a chance to see and fill the void. The metal parts spray paint shop picked up by one urban CDC has returned better than 10 percent from the beginning, reflecting a low purchasing price rather than improved operation. It is possible that this business would not have found a buyer in the absence of the CDC, in which case the market would surely have been imperfect.

Food co-ops are beginning to be a real threat to over-packaged, over-advertised, over-manicured supermarkets. The markets are responding by cutting frills. But the large, organic, bulk-packaging places are not co-ops; they are entrepreneurial establishments. Erewhon, which started as a market in Boston, now is a national distributor of organic foods. Celestial Seasonings started when a group of summer vacationers concocted a tea from berries, the now-famous Red Zinger. These are not stories of community enterprises but of traditional capitalism.

Finally, the worker-ownership movement has also been motivated more from internalizing some costs which are external to private capital (such as the cost of unemployment) and monetizing internal nonmonetary costs (especially safety), than from sensing missed opportunities for profit. A tannery in Peabody, Massachusetts was a missed opportunity, but the former workers who now own it do so as capitalists; current workers are workers, not owners. The GAF asbestos mine in Vermont, which was sold to the workers, was financed by Vermont banks because the state showed, in a study of the *secondary* effects of losing the wage income and production purchasing, that the state's economy and eventually the banks would suffer if they did not finance it, not that it was a good investment on its private merits. That GAF failed to forecast the rise in the price of asbestos demonstrates that they made a mistake, but the worker-owner movement had no better price forecasts and was not motivated by anticipated profits.

A market imperfection argument is based on the premise that people close to the action can see opportunities which the more distant owners of capital do not see. The brief review above indicates that though this is sometimes the case, it usually has to do with proximity, not with community. There are two modifications which deserve mention. One is that a low return to one party may be a high return to another. I would like to see a study of the uses made of the 3,000 A & P stores being closed in an efficiency drive. Two that I know of, in Cambridge, Mass., are now grocery stores. They seem to be doing well—but better than they did as A & P? Possibly so, but just as possibly the local entrepreneurs are getting the highest return they can, while the owners of A & P are increasing their returns also. Again, this argues that although local people may see missed opportunities, or consider situations as opportunities for themselves when they are not opportunities for others, it is the localness, not the communityness, which produces this. Obviously in the cases reported above, the local entrepreneurs were able to get financing, so the banks, also, saw the opportunity which A & P did not wish to exploit.

The first modification to the notion of market imperfections as a rationale for community enterprise, then, is that there are frictions in the system which create different capital markets, so that national capital deliberately shuns profitable opportunities in particular localities. This could easily be true in many urban areas. It speaks to improvements in entrepreneurial finance—and perhaps a national capital-allocation policy—but not to community control.

The second modification asks whether the return to the activity is the same when outsiders are owners. This is a strong argument for worker-ownership, as one assumption is that workers will be more productive if they have ownership interests. Thus, there is not one rate of return to an enterprise independent of who owns it but different rates which depend on ownership. The capital market is correct to leave, and workers are correct to purchase. This is a potentially powerful argument. It says that by restructuring the ownership of a stock of physical capital, the capi-

tal can become more productive. The new owners of the former
A & P groceries may be putting in more hours for less return than
A & P managers ever would. In terms of real resources, changing
the form of ownership may get you something for nothing.

There is a lot of implicit evidence that ordinary processes in
our system do generate this problem. Braverman, for example,
argues that monopoly capitalism deliberately takes knowledge of
production away from workers, creating managers as the possess-
ors of this knowledge and determiners of its use.[4] Workers fight
back, withholding their knowledge from the system. Therefore,
workers know how they could be more productive if they had an
incentive to be. That incentive might be ownership. Where capitalism has succeeded, then, it has imposed a loss on us in exchange
for redistributing more of the lower average proceeds to owners.
Though that may be a powerful theoretical indictment of the
capitalist system, it remains to be seen whether workers actually
have the ability to increase the productivity of capital through
alternative forms of ownership.[5]

Obviously this, too, needs to be studied. Specifically, if worker
ownership increases productivity, then a strong argument can be
made for worker ownership in a development plan. What rational
planner would sacrifice a percentage point rise in income to
preserve an imperfect capital market? Indeed, any legal form
which increases the output from a given set of resources should be
favored. Capital markets would indeed be imperfect if they operate to lower the return to capital from what it could be under
different forms of ownership.

A CATEGORIZATION OF MARKET
FAILURES

Based on this discussion of two basic kinds of market imperfections, I have defined four kinds of market failure relevant to
considering the function of community groups in capital placement:[6]

1) Market Failure One (MF One) occurs when the capital market
fails to place capital where it makes a maximum internal-monetary
return, through ignorance of the opportunity.

2) Market Failure Two (MF Two) occurs when the capital market

does maximize internal-monetary return, but by other criteria (the other three costs of production) the capital allocation is "wrong."

3) Market Failure Three (MF Three) occurs when the capital market is aware of opportunities to increase its internal-monetary return but is constrained from doing so.

4) Market Failure Four (MF Four) occurs when the capital, whether maximizing only internal-monetary return or social return, given the resources available to it, fails to produce the return it would, without additional cost, through a change in some legal form such as ownership control.

An analysis of which market failure, or what combination of failures, is occurring in a particular urban area is vital to the determination of corrective policies. I will provide evidence that community groups have no advantage in correcting MF One. Community groups have a definite advantage in correcting MF Two, but because this failure implies deficit finance, a plan for subsidization must accompany community efforts to overcome MF Two. MF Three usually requires some governmental powers, especially planning and land acquisition. Sometimes, as at the Quincy Market in Boston, the government does step in, coordinate, take the requisite amount of land, and do something which, piecemeal, would not pay. On the other hand, it is easy to claim that MF Three is the problem, while failing to see that a particular solution creates an MF Two situation. Urban renewal did this. Local governments are empowered and mandated to act in MF Three situations, but where they do so to the detriment of community residents, an argument can be made for community group involvement. Under MF Four, capital owners are not constrained by size or laws from putting a package together which they know would produce a maximum return. This imperfection says the wrong people own the capital, from the point of view of bringing out resources which do not want to work (or don't want to maximize productivity) for current capital owners.[7] The failure itself asks for examination of proposed solutions to urban underdevelopment, in terms of the relevant actors in a development plan. It suggests that *participants* in a project should acquire some of the benefits of ownership. This is clearly community control if "community" is appropriately defined. Even under more common definitions there may be a rule uniquely played by community groups in redressing Market Failure Four.

COMMUNITY-BASED GROUPS

These four market failures are just an expansion of the principle that a claim of error in capital allocation must either assert an imperfect capital market according to its own rules, or assert that its rules, however perfectly carried out, create the wrong results. The task now is to look at community-based groups (CBGs) and ask where their activities fit into this categorization of market failures. I briefly ran through several of the kinds of groups which fit under the general title CBG: CDCs, co-ops, worker-owned firms. One other movement should be added: the movement for decentralized government, or neighborhood government. Clearly MF Three will lead us to consider what kinds of governmental powers might best be exercised at what levels of government, but an extensive discussion of MF Three in relation to the neighborhood government movement would take us far afield of our purposes here.

I have attempted to categorize community groups by their origin, to see if the initial thrust of a group implies which areas of market failure the group will be best suited to attack. By and large this attempt does not lead to strong conclusions. There does seem to be a tie-in between one of the ways in which groups originate and their ability to pursue development activities. This involves a new argument, which I will make and then merge with the analysis of market failure.

I see four ways in which CBGs have originated 1) issue oriented, 2) charismatic leader, 3) institutional basis, 4) government program. I will give some examples of these different origins, and ask if one can determine from its origins how a community-based development group will fare, or which type of market failure it is trying to correct.

Issue-oriented CBGs are easily the most interesting. It should be obvious to anyone who has had anything to do with organizing that the interest and energy of people will come together over very limited, directed issues more easily than over large generalities. Consumers of all classes will organize to boycott meat, or protest utility rate increases, but a general organization to monitor prices, such as a Public Interest Research Group is inherently middle class, with voluntary participation limited mostly to youth. FIGHT in Rochester was established to protest racial discrimination in hiring at Xerox Corporation, not discrimination in general.

It won support in the form of guaranteed contracts from Xerox Corporation for an electronics plant which employed community residents. North Lawndale Economic Development Corporation crystallized to stop plans being formulated by Chicago for developing the Lawndale section of the city. Lummi Indian Tribal Enterprises was built from the beginning on the idea of developing acquaculture, the Lummis being a coastal tribe. The two best examples of single-issue organizations are probably Peoples Development Corporation of the Bronx, and the East 11th Street Project in Manhattan. In both cases abandoned apartment houses were taken over by squatters, renovated, purchased from the city for one dollar, and are now lived in by the people who rebuilt them. In both cases attention was paid to solar generation of heat and electricity, insulation, and so on. Simply because both capital and continuing costs were internal to the production process, better decisions were made. Owners who do not live in the houses do not have the same incentive to insulate, for they do not pay the heating bills. Absentee owners probably could not have brought the same amount of resources to bear, either. People would not have worked so hard either for someone else or for an abstraction. A similar project in Chicago includes rooftop vegetable greenhouses. These housing rehabilitations are probably excellent examples of correcting MF Four: the bringing forth of new productive resources by changing the form of ownership and community participation.

The obvious example of the charismatic leader is Reverend Leon Sullivan in Philadelphia. The Zion Corporation was open only to church members for its first six years, struggling under the 10/36 plan ($10 a month for 36 months) to self-finance development. It was opened to the public in 1968 and has received considerable support from the Ford Foundation since. But despite the favorable press and undoubted benefits it has created, no evaluation of Zion has demonstrated generation of any notable development. Similarly, the Hough Area Development Corporation in Cleveland was founded by DeForest Brown, another minister who realized that religion was insufficient to solve the people's problems. HADC was quickly funded by the Special Impact Program (now Title VII of the Community Services Act), which provided institutional support and equity capital for a shopping plaza, a housing complex, and an injection-molded rubber and plastic parts plant. Unlike Zion, HADC's founder moved on.

Through 1976 the injection-molding plant has lost over $900,000, though this is about the same level of capital loss it had sustained by the middle of 1974. HADC, being a general development corporation, has invested in different areas, including two MacDonalds and a maintenance service. In no area has it shown much success, as defined by normal business criteria, and the CDC is in trouble with its funding agency.

A number of groups seem to have come from different institutions which were looking for ways to increase community control or, by an alternative interpretation, ways to defuse the recognition by poor communities that lack of ownership keeps them on the sidelines of the capitalist economic system. Harlem Commonwealth Council was supported by Columbia University and The New School for Social Research. Bedford Stuyvesant Restoration Corporation is considered the creature of Bobby Kennedy and Jacob Javits, not of Franklin Thomas, its first and long-time president; IBM and the Ford Foundation provided the initial support. TELACU in East Los Angeles was started by the United Auto Workers. The Roxbury Action Project in Boston received early general support from the American Friends Service Committee. Its development attempts have included housing and businesses, with some important political success but limited development success.

In none of these cases is the indigenous leadership to be ignored. Somebody had to be there to get the money and run the organization. But the institutional support in these cases was critical to the very existence of the groups. This cannot be said of either Zion or HADC, or the Woodlawn Organization, or others which became critically different when large funding arrived but probably would not have died without it.

The government has been fundamental to the origin and survival of many community-based development groups. The Model Cities Program put perhaps $50 million into such groups. EDA has supported many community organizations. CSA, through the Community Action Program, has supported local development groups. Indeed, half of the Community Development Corporations funded under Title VII of the Community Services Act today were started by Community Action Agencies funded under Title II of the Act. Through fiscal 1976, Title VII has put over $150 million into urban CDCs, of which approximately two-thirds, over $100 million, was intended to be venture equity.

The evidence presented here, and indeed all the evidence I have been able to gather, will not support strong conclusions about the relationship of the origin of a group and its operations. Groups live beyond and, eventually, independent of their founding history. Nonetheless, I am willing to posit two conclusions which would be better looked at as hypotheses:

1) The more issue oriented the group, the more specific and limited the definition of the issue, the more likely will be the group's accomplishment of a development objective.
2) The more specific and limited the issue, the more likely it is that the group will structure itself to understand and correct market failures. The more general the objectives of the group, the more it will define success in MF One terms and fail thereby.

Groups which are started as general development groups, with more external private or government finance than internal volunteer help, will become successful only if they limit their objectives, aim toward specific outcomes, and plan these outcomes within the context of the ability of the group to survive and the ability of the project to attract community support.

If there is any validity to these observations, it reflects on two gaps which social scientists and political activists have failed to fill. One is a language which allows a community group to frame its activities within an explanation of why those activities are necessary. I believe my market failure analysis is a step in this direction. The other gap is an accounting system with which communities and potential funding sources could agree on the social benefits provided by the group's activities. If community groups attack Market Failure Two problems, an accounting system is required to determine if the gain is greater than the cost. The accounting system exists to do just that for MF One situations. It only half exists for MF Three situations, which is why large projects often do so much harm to specific populations. It does not satisfactorily describe MF Four situations (a correct accounting would add to public benefit any damage people would have done during time they would otherwise have had for themselves, which time is now added to the pool of resources).

It does seem that only those groups directed from the beginning toward MF Two issues can come to an MF Two strategy. The most directed groups aim at MF Four. Generalist groups are forced by lack of theory, lack of language, and lack of accounting, to attempt to redress only the failure of the capital market to find those few profitable opportunities which may still exist in depressed neighborhoods of central cities.

A BRIEF SUMMATION

At this stage, much of my comparison of different types of community organization is largely conjecture, since data are very difficult to come by. But the basis of an answer to the question, "What is the role of community-based development groups in urban development?" has been presented, and I want to summarize to this point before examining some figures I have been able to put together.

I presented the argument that development is capital placement and that the capital market is traditionally considered to work well. A development policy, as opposed to laissez-faire development, implies an objection to current operation of the capital market. I contend that the failure of development programs is due to the lack of articulation of the reasons that the private capital market does not work. I did not discuss the question of the aggregate quantity of capital, because surely if we are only concerned with how much capital there is, not how the capital is allocated, we cannot even define problems as "urban," or in any other locational context. We are concerned with where capital goes, what form the physical capital takes, and whether there is a relationship between the legal aspects of the capital— who own it, who controls it, etc.—and the return which can be obtained from it.

Capital placement by the private market can only be wrong if the market has imperfections, it doesn't play by its own rules; or if a perfect market does not yield the best solutions to the capital placement problems, its rules, when followed, turn out to be wrong. I further broke down the first of these propositions into failure to follow the rules because of a lack of information (Market Failure One) or because of frictions or restrictions on playing the game (Market Failure Three). Market Failure Two is the case where the rules go awry, when external or nonmonetary costs, in any combination, become large relative to the internal monetary costs of production, the only costs the capital market typically counts. Market Failure Four occurs when some resources fail to be supplied to the capital because the form of ownership or control of the production process does not induce those resources into the production system.

I presented a sketchy argument that benefits claimed for community groups in solving instances of Market Failure One can better be seen as reasons for developing local capital markets. The ability to see hidden profitable opportunities lies in individuals who may need technical assistance and capital finance, but there is no clear theoretical or empirical reason why CBGs need be involved. I will continue to emphasize that whatever CBGs are good at, it is not correcting MF One. I am much less sure what to say about the other market failures.

I then briefly described four ways in which community-based development organizations seem to have gotten started: around specific issues with proposed solutions, around a charismatic leader who promises to find solutions to general problems, from external institutional support in response to general problems, or from government programs similarly motivated. If articulating the problem is the first step toward a solution, one can look only to the limited issue-oriented groups for guidance.

My contention is that most community development groups are doing the wrong things, playing the wrong game, and being rewarded or penalized according to a set of rules which do not induce these groups to solve those market failures they could solve. I hope it is clear that I am not casting blame here. I am in awe of charismatic leaders. I laud the good intentions of private institutions and government programs. I am happy for those people employed in the few community-based business ventures which survive. However, none of that leads to a role for community-based groups in a rational urban development policy. What will lead to such a role is their ability to solve market failures.

The heart of the argument is that community groups have no advantage in solving Market Failure One. They do have an advantage in solving Market Failure Two, because costs external to the firm are imposed on the community. Community groups naturally include these costs in their calculations, or would if there were an accounting system and reward system for doing so. A development plan has to understand what failures there are, in what amount, and find the best institutional arrangements to solve them. The Special Impact Program (SIP) has implicitly chosen to see the problem as dominated by MF One. It stands as an important example of exactly the wrong approach to community-based groups. I will demonstrate that the SIP administrators are asking CDCs to solve MF One problems and that by this standard they are overwhelmingly failures.

THE SPECIAL IMPACT PROGRAM

The Rules

The rules of the Special Impact Program game are very simple. They are found in CSA Instruction 6158-1, effective November 3, 1975. One might ask what the rules were for the first seven years of the program, but I think the history of Instruction 6158-1, which I will not go into here, would indicate that this was very much a formalization of rules already in effect, as agreed to, by and large, by the CDCs as well as the administering agency. One could argue that the CDCs were formed and supported so they would agree with these rules, but that is just redistributing blame, which is not of much interest.

The Instruction says the program shall be considered "essentially a *demonstration* program" since the funding, which has never reached $50 million a year, hardly indicates a national development effort. CDCs fund two types of ventures: business and social. The social ventures are expected to require continued subsidy, though a good deal of emphasis is placed on getting that from other federal programs. Business ventures are expected to be self-sufficient—that is, even if they do not make money, they should not lose it. Thus "business ventures," which are clearly the bulk of ventures, have a minimum private internal return of zero. As in pool, they have to call their shot: they are not supposed to say "it is a social venture" only after they learn it is losing money.

The Instruction describes profit "optimization" in vague language which does at least recognize that there are community benefits which might not show up on income statements. But it is not good enough to get the ball in the pocket off two side cushions if one calls for a straight shot. If the venture is not going to maximize profit, say so up front, and say what benefits will be provided for the community in place of profits. Though these are the ways the game *can* be played, the way it *should* be played is clearly stated:

> Although it is appropriate for a given CDC to have a mix of venture types, the priority over the short term should be on business ventures. Moreover, among business ventures, the priority over the short term should be on profit maximization, rather than optimization.

The Instruction concludes by noting that although other benefits, such as employment and human development, are nice things to have, the CDC is really not expected to do much about all that.

There is really no question that, though the language is designed to cover a multitude of *ex post facto* sins, Market Failure One is assumed. There *are* internal-monetary return opportunities out there, exactly the kinds of returns the private capital market looks for. Find those opportunities, follow good business practices, and the community will develop.

There might be room in these rules for ventures which make profits which are positive but below rates acceptable to the private capital market. As discussed above, besides worker-ownership, there already is an institution prepared to do that: the proprietor who works harder than a manager would. Indeed, many CDCs respond to the directions by finding proprietors to lend money to or to joint venture with. Thus, if the Instruction is broader than MF One, it includes MF Four. The important point is that correcting MF Two situations is specifically denied as the purpose of the program.

Not Following The Rules

I have the feeling that community groups can often rise above silly rules. My problem, as a researcher, is that the information I get is generated *by* the rules. Thus the best information I have—and none too good at that—is income statements and balance sheets from ventures. Once the name of the game is "business as usual," it is clear what data to collect. Since I think that is exactly the

wrong game, I am often frustrated in attempts to find evidence
which would pertain to market failures other than MF One. Once
again, the lack of social accounting leads to inability to know what
some groups really do.

I do know, however, that the CDC Board in Denver discussed
the issue of selling Coors Beer in its supermarkets. The impact
area population is mostly Mexican-American and the position and
practices of the Coors family are well enough known that I think I
am not disclosing secret information in saying the Board was dis-
turbed at its implicit support thereof. Neither can it be a secret
that the Board voted to take the product off its shelves. Had this
action been the result of consumer protests, as was the case in
many markets over the grape boycott, one would think nothing of
it. Just more profit maximization. But the initiative came from the
Board, not from the streets. This action shows that community-
based businesses can make different decisions, decisions based on
some large concept of "community" and an overt reaction to the
costs imposed on that community by a particular production
process. But now we must turn to the more usual picture.

Following The Rules

One hundred thirty-six ventures funded by the Special Impact
Program CDCs were alive at some time in the year July 1, 1974
through June 30, 1975. Of these, I could get profit/loss data on
103. Of these, over 70 percent showed losses, although ventures
with profits in the most recent quarter, even if insufficient to
cover previous losses within the year, were considered "profitable"
for this count. This was a depression year, so it is hard to know
what to expect. But among CDC start-up ventures, 32 percent of
those started in 1973 or later were profitable, whereas only 17
percent of those started earlier were currently profitable. If the
depression was the major detriment to success, the older ventures
would be expected to fare better. Of businesses started elsewhere
and acquired by a CDC, 36 percent were profitable in this 12-
month period.

I could get data for a full 12 months on only 26 ventures.
Some of the ventures, of course, either opened or closed in this

period, and therefore, would not have 12-month data; but the basic problem is the pitiful inattention paid to data gathering for this program. Four ventures in real estate had a total one-year loss of $31,500, on an SIP equity of $2.320 million. Four non-real estate ventures, on which I could find no employment information, had a total one-year loss of $85,000 on an SIP equity of $360,000, with additional capital in the form of loans from the sponsoring CDC of $79,000. The 18 remaining ventures had a total one-year loss of $1.587 million on a combined SIP equity and loans of $5.580 million. These ventures employed 314.5 people (counting part-time as one-half person), for a capital cost of $17,741 per job.[8] Inflating that figure by 50 percent to account for the cost of the CDC (as noted, about two of each three dollars of grant funds is venture capital) would provide a very conservative measure of program cost per job, since it does not count ventures which were tried and failed. Nor does it count support and program administration funds. This conservative estimate is close to $27,000. If the ventures continue to lose money, then further injections of funds would be necessary to sustain them. Thus the money outlay from the government per job in the Special Impact Program cannot be precisely determined. It is distressing to calculate that the annual loss comes to over $5,000 per full-time equivalent employee. However, if the average wage was greater than this—and I do not have the figures—then on a flow basis the government did well. As sales in these 18 ventures were over $5 million, it is possible they contributed to the wage bill.

Other federal programs do not calculate the capital cost per job. The private sector does not capitalize the kinds of jobs CDC ventures provide at $27,000 per job, but then the private sector did not provide these jobs or it would not be an issue.[9] Thus, there is information on only a small sample of CDC ventures, and very little with which to compare it. The interesting point is that this may be a cheap way for the government to create jobs, which is what the rules say not to do. It is not a very good showing on profits, which is what the rules ask. If the government were to look for programs in which the total federal cost—calculated with appropriate discounts to cover expenditures at different points in time per job created—was minimal, the community-based venture approach might be in the running. Of course, then we would have to worry about how many of these 314 jobs were new, but I will not do that here.

What I conclude from this demonstration is that the CDCs may be good at doing something they are not asked to do: capitalize jobs which may require continuing subsidy, but where that subsidy is less than the wage bill generated thereby. However, they are forbidden from doing that—ventures must be self-sufficient. CDCs are not at all good at producing profits, at least they have not been so far. Given where they invest, though, who can say they are not maximizing? An implicit theory of Market Failure One, translated into a federal program which values capital over labor, profits over wage subsidies, provides no evidence at all that CDCs should be included in a development plan. However, that seems to be more the failure of the theory and the directions given to these groups than a failure of community groups themselves.

THE ROLE OF COMMUNITY GROUPS IN URBAN DEVELOPMENT

My view of the requisites for a successful urban development policy is obvious at this point. The first task is to define the problem in terms of the failure of traditional capital allocating mechanisms to put capital where we apparently agree it should go. If we conclude that there are currently desirable activities which are also profitable opportunities of feasible size, then we need to find the people who know about the opportunities and finance and assist them. I have not discussed the loan fund activities of community groups, but I can say that we do have data which we hope to investigate. Thus, whether community groups would be good financiers of entrepreneurial development under MF One is an open question. But community groups seem to have no advantage in doing it themselves.

Looking at the failures, we may conclude that the scale necessary for urban development is too large for private enterprise, or that even if private enterprise would be willing to undertake a massive scheme, there would be legal or political difficulties. Cities themselves ought to plan and develop large land areas, and city planning departments say they are doing just that. Yet certain neighborhoods seem systematically to be neglected. Thus, for example, there is no theoretical reason why the City of Chicago could not have amassed the land holdings of North Lawndale Economic Development Corporation (now Pyra-midwest Corporation) and planned its various activities and even received federal support. But the fact is the City of Chicago did not do these things, and the CDC did. Worse than that, the city was developing plans to suburbanize the Lawndale area, golf course and all, with the inevitable removal of current residents. In contrast, Pyramidwest explicitly acts to keep Lawndale "a community for the people who now live there and to redevelop that community for their use.[10] MF Three situations call for some interference with ordinary market processes. The argument for *community* involvement with MF Three situations, however, is the failure of city government, not the failure of the market.

How to internalize external costs, how to monetize nonmonetary costs, is well known. Only the federal government can successfully finance such internalization, if capital is free to move to places where *it* need not bear these costs. Indeed, even the federal government is limited, as capital now goes out of the country finding places where it can impose more costs of production on workers and communities, thereby imposing the even greater cost of nonproduction on the United States labor force. Market Failure Two puts the question squarely: what kind of capital allocation institution will actually do the right things? I am not convinced that any top-down government funded "community" group will make better decisions than private capital. But to the extent that costs are distributed from the firm to a definable "community" under ordinary private production, that community is the logical foundation for a new institution which can make better capital decisions. Federal finance of community groups is called for in MF Two situations, with the understanding that ventures of these groups may require continuing operating subsidy.

I am most impressed with specific issue groups which set clear, but limited objectives. A development program should have funds available for such groups, after they have demonstrated that they can accomplish something and that it is good. It takes no great calculation to realize that the saving of residential structures combined with training and employing a new labor force, as in

Bedford-Stuyvesant, is a worthwhile development activity well pursued by community groups. It is even more impressive, as in the Bronx and Manhattan, when resources are brought into play which were not even available to the labor market. A program demanding excessive individual contributions will limit itself to the middle class. But these projects can teach us much about what cash flow is required to keep the people in food, clothing, and shelter, while they still expend massive amounts of additional effort because the results are *theirs.*

CDCs argue that planning and administering require institutional support. My argument here is for more project support. Not support like Community Development Block Grants, which take community suggestions for city-directed projects. Cities do not know what to do with such funds. The new Urban Development Action Grants (UDAG) will be as fruitlessly expended as most CDBG funds, because they are not seeking to match specific problems with groups best suited to solve them. Some community groups are clearly in the best position to solve some urban problems. Reliance on community groups to solve problems they are not suited for, as in the past, will only serve to continue the fact and impression that community-based development fails.

WHAT NEXT?

I have read a number of program reviews and am almost always disappointed at the vagueness of the conclusions offered. For example, consider this review of the Model Cities Program:[11]

> Rather than discouraging the emergence of new structures, with new constituencies and new methods, we should encourage them by allocating a part of the federally funded program budgets explicitly for new organizations, including client organizations, which seek to develop radical as well as less radical alternatives to present agency structures and programs.

A call for project innovation puts the burden of thought on others, giving no reason other than differentness to fund a project. It demonstrates a failure to define the problem. Once defined as a series of related problems, "development" will lend itself to analysis. One task of the analysis is to relate the structure and incentive systems operating within an institution to the goals that institution is expected to attain. We should begin to see that certain kinds of institutions do some things well and should be asked to do those things when they are needed. Entrepreneurs will take care of MF One situations if there is finance and training available. Participant-owner groups will bring forth more resources than under traditional ownership. Community groups can articulate the costs imposed on them from ordinary production decisions, including the decision of capital to leave the area. But without an accounting system to measure these costs, and the reduction in them from the group's activities, there is no way to monitor the group and reward its success.

A development program is a capital placement program. An institutional incentive analysis based on market failure analysis can bring about rational support of the correct institutions to solve identified problems. Correct placement of capital in central cities involves a combination of entrepreneurial finance, large scale redevelopment projects with substantial community group involvement, community group direction of capital to solve cases where external and nonmonetary costs of traditional production are large, and participant ownership. A program which first identified the extent of the four market failures outlined above would then have to select proper institutions to fund, monitor these institutions, and create incentive systems for their behavior. I foresee no successful development programs without following these steps.

REFERENCES

[1] For example, see "Development of Capital Markets in the United States," *Business Review,* Federal Reserve Bank of Dallas, April 1976.

[2] Although some firms have devised social accounts, these are neither standardized nor widespread. Even where they are used, it is hard to see that the accounts are part of the firm's decision process, as opposed to an *ex post* rationale for whatever it decided to do on other grounds.

[3] A little arithmetic combined with elementary business knowledge will lead the reader quickly to realize that the wages paid on these jobs are low by urban standards. But they are rural wages where there were not earnings opoortunities before and are clearly benefits to the residents as well as to the entrepreneurs with whom Kentucky Highlands engages in joint ventures.

[4] Braverman, Harry, *Labor and Monopoly Capital* (New York: Monthly Review Press), 1974.

[5] A parallel argument, that utilization of consumption facilities depends on the form and ownership structure, is more common than the argument presented here about production. For example, "congruence between culture and organization maximizes the chance that medical services will be accessible and acceptable to consumers. Sick people must use medical services before those services can help them get well." Richard M. Hessler, "Citizen Participation, Social Organization, and Culture: A Neighborhood Health Center for Chicanos," 36 *Human Organization* 2, Summer, 1977, p. 125.

[6] For an earlier exposition of three of these categories of market failure in the context of setting optimal rules for Special Impact Program funded ventures, see Stephan Michelson, "On Profit Maximization by SIP Ventures," *CCED Newsletter,* June-July 1977.

[7] Though one can find analogies to the failures I depict in the traditional economic analysis of how markets might fail to maximize welfare, MF Four cannot be found in traditional expositions. This is because in traditional theory resources are fixed and respond to allocation demands only on the basis of price. Traditional solutions, therefore, are always concerned with sources and uses of funds and allocation of a fixed bundle of resources.

[8] This figure was calculated from unrounded totals.

[9] Total capitalization is greater than the SIP share. In general, SIP leveraging of venture capital has been at a rate of approximately one:one. Thus there is about $45,000 of capital cost per job, still below the national average for manufacturing,

but surely well above the average capitalization of comparable jobs. The figure in the text would be more relevant for
comparison with federal programs.

[10] North Lawndale Economic Development Corporation, *Proposal
for Refunding* (to OED/CSA) 1971-1972, April 1971.

[11] Warren, Roland L., "The Model Cities Program: An Assessment"
(The Social Welfare Forum), 1971. Reprinted in Spiegel,
Hans B.C., ed., *Citizen Participation in Urban Development*,
vol. III (Learning Resources Corporation), 1974, p. 42.

The Role of the City in the Region's Economy

CHAPTER ELEVEN

James E. Peterson*

THE PROBLEMS OF THE CENTRAL CITY

Over the past 20 years, this country has experienced rapid economic growth and increased urbanization. These trends, however, have been unevenly distributed. Many central cities have in fact, experienced significant declines in their population and economies, both in relative and in absolute terms.

The reduction in the central cities' economic base can be measured by losses in income, employment, population, and other factors. Between 1960 and 1970, the central cities of 18 of the 35 largest SMSAs lost population.[1] All 35 suburban areas had population gains that ranged from 4.4 percent to 134.7 percent. Of the 50 largest cities in the United States (population over 250,000), 40, including the five largest, lost in population between 1970 and 1975.

During the 1950s, central cities lost an average of 2,000 manufacturing jobs per year, much of it to their suburbs. In the decade that followed, central cities lost manufacturing jobs at an annual average of over 3,500. During these 20 years, the average annual loss for the 40 largest SMSAs was over 25,000 manufacturing jobs. Between 1960 and 1970, 13 central cities of the largest SMSAs had either a loss in jobs or no gain. In only one SMSA of the 35 did the suburbs show any loss and in every other case, the percent-

*James E. Peterson is Executive Director, National Council for Urban Economic Development.

age increase of jobs in the suburbs far outdistanced those in the central city.

Nor has the shift in jobs been solely those in manufacturing. Table 1 illustrates the locational changes of Fortune 500 companies in ten cities.

TABLE ONE.   Number of Fortune 500 Companies in Ten Cities, by City, Suburb, and Region, 1956 and 1971

City*	Central City			Suburbs			Region		
	1956	1971	Change	1956	1971	Change	1956	1971	Change
New York	140	116	−24	16	40	+24	156	156	0
Chicago	47	37	−10	4	15	+11	51	52	+1
Pittsburgh	22	15	−7	2	0	−2	24	15	−9
Detroit	18	8	−10	2	4	+2	20	12	−8
Cleveland	16	14	−2	0	2	+2	16	16	0
Philadelphia	14	9	−5	8	4	−4	22	13	−9
St. Louis	11	10	−1	1	0	−1	12	10	−2
Los Angeles	10	15	+5	5	6	+1	15	21	+6
San Francisco	8	7	−1	4	8	+4	12	15	+3
Boston	7	5	−2	2	2	0	9	7	−2
Total	293	236	−57	44	81	+37	337	317	−20

*The ten cities are ranked in the order of number of headquarters in 1956.

Source: Quante, Wolfgang, "The Relocation of Corporate Headquarters from New York City," Ph.D. dissertation, Columbia University, 1974.

While the ten cities lost 57 headquarters, their suburbs gained 37.

The most serious deterioration of the urban economic base has been occurring in the older Northeast and North Central cities. These changes in employment and population have altered the characteristics of the central city vis-à-vis their suburban rings. In addition to the shift in jobs and people, there has been a redistribution of income, wealth, and fiscal tax base between the older central cities and their suburbs.

Household income in the central cities is below that of their suburbs, as are property values. This is in marked contrast to the situation 20 years ago. The average household income in 1970 for 19 large northeastern cities was $10,325, compared with $14,098 in their surrounding suburbs. In 12 out of 15 Northeast and North Central SMSAs per capita property tax values were higher in the suburbs than the inner city. Sixteen percent of the households in the central cities of the Northeast had income below $3,000 in 1970. The figure for their respective regions was 9 percent. At the same time, only 33 percent of households in the central cities had incomes over $10,000, versus 46 percent for the suburbs.

The out-migration of economic activity and its middle class has created serious problems for the central city. Despite a weakened tax and economic base, the central cities have been trying to deal with deteriorating and vacant buildings, high crime and unemployment rates, a continued in-migration of the poor and immigrants, and increased demands for public services. These factors have precipitated today's "urban crisis," a convenient term for three kinds of problems which are basically a result of the economic decline of the central cities.

Any rigorous policy analysis requires that we understand and appreciate the differences in these problems. They are the problems of poverty, of the physical environment, and of the public economy.

The problems of poverty in this country are geographically centered in the cities. Of the approximately 25 million people with incomes below the poverty line, 25 percent of the indigent white and 44 percent of the indigent nonwhite live in central cities. The dispersal of employment opportunities to the suburbs, in conjunction with the lack of low-cost housing in the suburbs, has cut off the poor from the benefits of a growing economy. Unemployment rates in central cities have generally exceeded the national rate by a wide margin. While the unemployment rate nationally was 7.7 percent in 1976, the rate in nine out of the ten most distressed central cities was 10 percent, with rates in Detroit, New York, Philadelphia, and St. Louis over 11 percent.[3]

The physical environment in central cities often discourages economic growth. Younger cities have problems of acquiring necessary public facilities, while older cities have problems maintaining and restoring public facilities such as streets, sewage systems, water mains, and electric power distribution systems. Mature cities also suffer from the problems of congestion, noise, and air and water pollution. Because the suburbs do not share these difficulties to the extent of the central cities, and because of the availability of cheap suburban land easily accessible by highways, they continue to draw the major share of new economic activity.

The problems of the public economy in central cities are aggravated by the selective migration to the suburbs. The problems of poverty and those of the physical environment have put central cities in the dual bind of increasing service loads and decreasing revenue sources. The central cities must continually raise tax rates and seek new taxes to keep up with rising expenditures. These efforts have often been unsuccessful, requiring cities to rely even more on intergovernmental transfers.

Numerous studies have attempted to classify and quantify the degree of distress in the nation's urban areas. The studies invariably indicate that the most severe problems are concentrated in the nation's 57 central cities with population of 250,000 or more. Within that group, the older cities of the Northeast and Mideast are cited as being in a state of long-term decline and unable to deal with their problems without significant state and federal assistance.

A Brookings Institution study developed a composite index of central city distress using factors such as economic condition, population change, and age of housing.[4] This study found the incidence of hardship to be greatest in the larger cities, those with high minority populations, and those located in the Northeast region of the country.

In another study, a composite index was developed to express the relationship between the central city and its suburbs.[5] It was based on unemployment, education, income level, dependency, crowded housing, and poverty factors. The index was prepared for the 55 most populous cities in the country's 66 largest SMSAs in 1970. Only for 12 of the 55 did the cities index indicate that for the above six factors, they were better off than their suburbs. Furthermore, the results indicated that the cities with the greatest disadvantages in relation to their suburbs tended to be the older Northeast and North Central cities.

THE NECESSITY OF THE CENTRAL CITY

Acknowledging the fact that a number of the nation's central cities are experiencing severe problems of poverty, physical environment, and public finance, we might ask if we need the large central cities? Do they play a necessary role in the life and economy of the nation? The answers to these questions are yes. To abandon these cities to a policy of benign neglect is unthinkable.

The cities' role in the nation and in their regions, while declining, is nonetheless vital. First, they are still home to a large portion of the population. The 27 cities with over 500,000 in population constitute 15 percent of the nation's total population. The 375 SMSA central cities include 31 percent of the country's people.

As Table 2 indicates, central cities still are a large and important employment center for the regional work force. Of the 25 SMSAs listed, central cities provide the work place for 18.8-44.7 percent of their suburban populations. On the whole, 30 percent of those living outside the city work in the central city.

Central cities often remain the cultural, service, and transportation centers for their regions, though declining in importance in this respect.

The central cities have a new role in this era of greater environmental and energy concerns and of high costs and impacts of development. In a recent report to the House Committee on Banking, Finance and Urban Affairs, Congressman Henry Reuss argues that the new vital function of central cities is as the "Great Conservator of Land, Energy and Resources."[6]

The discontinuous, low-density development typical of suburban areas is damaging to air and water quality and encourages erosion and flooding. The most severe problem, however, is that it destroys needed agricultural land. Over 2 million acres of serviceable cropland are lost every year and an additional 2 million acres are "isolated."

Increased development diminishes our limited land resources.

> Between now and the end of this century, the statisticians say we will build as much again as we have built in our entire history. Every 10 years new homes and apartment houses, schools and hospitals, factories and offices, roads and railroads, shops and parking lots, gas stations and whatever will cover some 5 million acres, an area the size of New Jersey.[7]

According to the Reuss report:

> Sprawl development is wasteful of energy in several ways: In transportation, in heat loss, in the energy-intensive activity of building new physical structures and facilities, and in the energy loss represented by abandoning and demolishing structures in the central city.[8]

TABLE TWO. Place of Work for SMSAs With Work Force of 500,000 or More, 1970*

Area	Total Work Force† Number	Living Inside Central City									Living Outside Central City								
		Number	Percent of SMSA Work Force	Working Inside Central City	Percent Resident Work Force	Working Elsewhere in SMSA	Percent	Outside SMSA	Percent	Unreported	Number	Percent of SMSA Work Force	Working Inside Central City	Percent Resident Work Force	In SMSA Outside Central City	Percent	Outside SMSA	Percent	Unreported
Anaheim, Cal.	536	171	31.9	78.5	45.9	49.0	28.7	33.3	19.5	10.4	365	68.1	68.7	18.8	176.2	48.2	102.1	28.0	18.2
Atlanta	577	204	35.4	140.5	68.8	37.5	18.4	2.9	1.4	22.7	373	64.6	146.2	39.2	196.2	52.6	10.4	2.8	20.2
Baltimore	814	343	42.1	229.9	67.0	72.5	21.1	5.7	1.7	34.5	471	57.9	135.9	28.9	279.7	59.4	29.5	6.3	25.9
Boston	1,111	258	23.2	176.4	68.4	49.5	19.2	6.4	2.5	25.7	853	76.8	195.7	22.9	556.8	65.3	45.1	5.3	55.1
Chicago	2,790	1,336	47.9	988.0	74.0	205.7	15.4	17.5	1.3	124.9	1,454	52.1	354.4	24.4	978.8	67.3	37.5	2.6	83.6
Cincinnati	510	171	33.5	115.3	67.5	39.1	22.9	4.0	2.3	12.3	340	66.7	118.6	34.9	183.2	53.9	23.6	6.9	14.2
Cleveland	798	277	34.7	183.8	66.4	59.9	21.6	3.4	1.2	29.5	521	65.3	205.8	39.5	269.7	51.8	21.9	4.2	23.9
Dallas	647	362	55.9	287.0	79.0	36.4	10.1	7.9	2.2	31.1	284	43.9	127.0	44.7	131.3	46.2	11.5	4.0	14.3
Detroit	1,509	533	35.3	317.6	59.6	160.6	30.1	7.2	1.4	47.6	976	64.7	215.8	22.1	685.2	70.2	28.3	2.9	46.8
Houston	780	504	64.6	414.5	82.2	40.9	8.1	5.4	1.1	42.7	276	35.4	118.5	42.9	135.0	48.9	7.6	2.8	15.1
Kansas City, Mo.	511	209	40.9	144.0	68.9	36.8	17.6	3.7	1.8	24.6	302	59.1	112.7	37.3	161.7	53.5	8.0	2.6	19.8
Los Angeles-Long Beach	2,740	1,260	46.1	841.9	66.8	295.7	23.5	25.2	2.0	97.6	1,480	54.0	420.5	28.4	910.8	61.5	53.5	3.6	94.9
Miami	501	144	28.7	73.5	51.0	52.9	36.7	3.3	2.3	14.1	357	71.3	101.2	28.3	213.3	59.7	14.2	4.0	28.2
Milwaukee	557	291	52.2	202.5	69.6	63.0	21.6	3.7	1.3	22.3	266	47.8	89.0	35.5	157.8	59.3	7.5	2.8	11.2
Minneapolis-St. Paul	731	312	42.7	233.1	74.7	57.3	18.4	2.8	0.9	18.9	419	57.3	171.9	41.0	233.0	53.2	7.9	1.9	16.0
New York City	4,474	3,094	69.1	2,542.3	82.2	98.9	3.2	119.4	3.9	333.6	1,380	30.8	335.4	24.3	883.1	64.0	68.2	4.9	93.0
Newark	739	130	17.6	66.2	50.9	33.1	25.5	18.6	14.3	12.0	609	82.4	70.8	11.6	381.6	62.7	115.6	19.0	41.1
Paterson-Clifton-Passaic	561	115	20.5	58.0	50.4	28.2	24.5	15.5	13.5	12.9	447	79.7	34.3	7.7	247.0	55.3	142.6	31.9	22.8
Philadelphia	1,849	737	39.9	557.0	75.5	80.1	10.9	16.3	2.2	83.9	1,112	60.1	212.2	19.1	736.7	66.3	81.3	7.3	81.9
Pittsburgh	846	187	22.1	137.9	73.8	35.2	18.8	1.9	1.0	11.9	660	78.0	146.9	22.3	460.7	69.8	19.3	2.9	32.8
St. Louis	876	223	25.5	157.2	70.5	42.1	18.9	1.4	0.6	22.8	653	74.5	181.5	27.8	422.8	64.7	10.8	1.7	37.5
San Diego	540	283	52.4	220.9	78.1	39.6	14.0	3.6	1.3	18.4	257	47.6	81.3	31.6	155.6	60.5	4.4	1.7	15.8
San Francisco	1,253	457	36.5	346.0	75.9	56.7	12.4	7.6	1.7	46.4	796	63.5	208.4	26.2	493.9	62.0	41.7	5.2	52.1
Seattle	538	239	44.4	193.8	81.1	28.4	11.9	3.8	1.6	13.4	299	55.6	127.5	42.6	148.1	49.5	9.2	3.1	13.9
Washington, D.C.	1,230	334	27.1	219.5	65.7	53.0	15.9	4.1	1.2	57.1	896	72.8	271.2	30.3	537.0	59.9	30.3	3.4	57.4

*Coleman, William G., The Future of Cities: Contrasting Strategies for the Haves and Have Nots, prepared for Conference on Reorganization, Woodrow Wilson International Center for Scholars, Smithsonian Institution, Washington, D.C., September 19-20, 1977.

†Numbers of persons in thousands.

Source: U.S. Bureau of the Census, U.S. Census of Population: 1970, Detailed Population Characteristics, U.S. Summary (Washington, D.C.: Government Printing Office, 1973), pp. 1877-78.

Citing a 1974 study sponsored jointly by HUD, CED, and EPA titled, "The Cost of Sprawl," the Reuss report continues by noting the higher cost of operating and maintaining the typical suburban development. In the higher density central city, transportation construction is 26 percent cheaper, school construction 31 percent cheaper, and utility construction 17 percent cheaper. Reinvestment and re-use of the facilities of the central cities can ultimately save energy, resources, and development costs.

The role of the city, however, is not limited to that of an environmental one. Central cities have traditionally been the source for new, innovative, and growing industries which provide the basis for the economic health of the entire region. Innovative and newly established firms continue to rely on central city location during their incubation period. Without the high density of labor skills, transportation, capital, and the economies of scale provided by large central cities, it is doubtful if the entrepreneur of the 1970s will be capable of establishing the growth industries of the last third of the 20th century.

Large central cities have historically been a significant factor in allowing large groups of poor to upgrade themselves and join the economic mainstream. A substantial supply of very low-cost housing, in proximity to a variety of low-skilled jobs, has allowed successive waves of immigrants gradually to improve their financial conditions. Despite their loss of manufacturing jobs, central cities are continuing to be the home of the poor and immigrants.

THE THEORIES OF ECONOMIC BASE

The growth of many suburban areas has been financially subsidized by numerous federal programs which have had the effect of using the traditional economic wealth of central cities to help build suburban areas. A recent report by the Rand Corporation cites federal tax subsidies to homeownership, construction of the interstate highway system, and subsidies for the construction of water and waste treatment plants as having played a major part in the suburbanization of both industry and population. Federal energy policy has favored economic growth in the South, and funding programs for the construction of economic infrastructure have encouraged growth in expanding areas at the expense of the country's older cities.[9]

Many of the large central cities, in response to their problems, are undertaking comprehensive programs to consciously revitalize their economies. Most of these programs are based upon the concepts of the traditional economic base theory which relies on private sector employment as the principle measure and method of economic stability.

The economic base concept implies a quantitive relationship between urban and regional growth. Local economic activity is classified into two components: basic activity, or goods and services that are produced for export to the region, and nonbasic activity, or goods and services produced for local consumption. Local growth depends on basic activity which, through the multiplier effect, creates employment and income impacts. Manufacturing is usually the urban area's primary basic activity; therefore, changes in the demand for manufacturing output will lead to multiple changes in both income and employment.

The growth of the metropolitan region depends on the area's mix of export functions—the more diversified, the better. As manufacturing has become increasingly freed from its resource base and market orientation, urban centers have lost much of their growth-producing basic activity.

The traditional economic theory has limitations which may prevent it from providing a reasonable basis for developing policies for the economic revitalization of older central cities. It is a demand-driven model which focuses upon changes in the external demand for a city's exportable products. The city has often little or no control over this variable. The theory also downplays the fact that as a city grows and matures in size, there is a tendency toward greater self-sufficiency and increased trading among various sectors within the city's economy. Internal demand for goods and services produces growth as well. Finally, economic base theory has difficulty in differentiating among export industries. Increases in some activity may generate far greater impacts than similar increases in other firms.

In the short run, employment and income respond to the current mix of activities, but the mix changes over time. In the long run, growth and vitality of an urban economy rest on its capacity to invest and innovate. In this perspective, the real eco-

nomic base of the city is the relative cost and creativity of its local
economic activities.

THE FEDERAL URBAN POLICY

The Carter administration is presently shaping its own federal
urban policy. As reported in *The New York Times* the policy is
based upon "promoting economic development of the nation's
ailing big cities, rather than on starting ambitious new social
programs." Under consideration are several major proposals.

The major thrust of the policy is to create jobs, mostly in the
private sector. To achieve this objective the creation of an Urban
Development Bank has been proposed. This agency will provide
grants and low interest loans to encourage businesses to locate
and/or remain in the city. Also proposed is the use of tax incentives to make it worthwhile for the private sector to reinvest in
the central city.

Other major elements that are under consideration include:
1) Using federal funds as incentives to get better cooperation and
performance from local governments and better cooperation
between central cities and their suburbs. 2) Coordinating fragmented federal programs and practices and shifting them from
their traditional antiurban bias. 3) Antiredlining proposals and the
creation of a secondary market for mortgages to encourage the
middle class to remain in the city.

COMPONENTS OF A NATIONAL URBAN
POLICY

The Administration's urban policy is commendable as far as it
goes, but there are several areas in which it is deficient. The thrust
of the new policy is to create new jobs, primarily in the private
sector, through the use of financial incentives to encourage new
investment in central cities. The ultimate test of the incentive
strategy will be whether the incentives are large enough to overcome the original cost differential and disadvantages to business

remaining in the central city. The Administration is likely to discover that the cost differential is substantial and that incentives alone will have marginal impact.

Over the long run, an effective federal strategy must include helping central cities to build a capacity for economic development. Many cities are still in the early stages of creating economic development programs and lack the staff and planning capability necessary for effective local programs. Just as crucial for local governments is creating the capacity for public/private cooperation. Federal incentives without developing these capacities may prove to be insufficient.

The national urban policy must recognize the fact that for large, mature central cities, the kind experiencing the most severe distress, internal trading and interdependence may be at least as important as the traditional economic base. Therefore, the city's capacity to invest and innovate must be expanded. Federal assistance must be reoriented toward problems rather than being project specific. Furthermore, available federal tools should be permitted to be packaged and for long-term commitment they should be made to reflect the needs and realities of urban development activities.

Federal efforts toward greater central city/suburban cooperation must be made to produce meaningful results. Previous attempts to promote cooperation have resulted in regional plans and, in some instances, in actual regional program cooperation. Too often, though, the conflicts between inner city and suburbs continue. The federal government, through its methods of grants administration, has fostered much of this competition.

Finally, the Administration's urban policy must be cognizant of the complex governmental structure in which our cities exist. The Brookings Institution study previously cited concluded:

> To a significant degree, the social and economic hardship conditions of central cities are a function of governmental structure. Often regarded as a dull subject and relegated to the academic sidelines, the examination of governmental structure in relation to economic and social conditions is essential for understanding and dealing with urban needs.[10]

Thus, a federal proposal to review the government's traditionally antiurban bias is a necessary and correct first step. Another step would be to define the federal government's role in helping central cities find their new position in the metropolitan economy.

REFERENCES

[1] Sacks, Seymour, "The City as a Center of Employment," paper delivered to the Conference on Urban Governance of the Joint Center for Political Studies, Washington, D.C., April 10, 1975, taken from *To Save A City,* Congressman Henry S. Reuss, Subcommittee on the City, 95th Cong., 1st Sess., Washington, D.C., p. 2.

[2] Vaughan, Roger J., *The Urban Impacts of Federal Policies,* vol. 2, *Economic Development* (Santa Monica, Calif.: Rand Corp.), 1977, p. 19.

[3] Reuss, *op. cit.* p. 13.

[4] Pechman, Joseph A., ed., *Setting National Priorities: The 1978 Budget* (Washington, D.C.: Brookings Institution), 1977, p. 287.

[5] Nathan, Richard P. and Adams, Charles, *Understanding Central City Hardship* (Washington, D.C.: Brookings Institution), 1976, pp. 49-53.

[6] Reuss, *op. cit.*

[7] Editorial from *The Washington Post,* November 20, 1971, taken from *National Land Use Policy.* Printed for the use of the Committee on Interior and Insular Affairs, 92nd Cong., 2nd Sess., April 1972, Washington, D.C., p. 21.

[8] Reuss, *op. cit.,* p. 18.

[9] Vaughan, *op. cit.,* p. 126.

[10] Nathan, *op. cit.,* p. 60.

The Scope for Local Government Action

CHAPTER TWELVE

Gail Garfield Schwartz*

Economic development gained priority status among local governmental policy issues as a direct consequence of the dual recessions of the 1970s. In most cities, unemployment rates were more than twice the level normally considered tolerable, and they were higher by far in the cities than in nonmetropolitan areas. In northeastern and some midwestern cities the economic decline severely exacerbated growing fiscal crises. In western cities, the falloff in aerospace contracts underscored the need to diversify the urban economy. The reality of resource scarcity hit home dramatically with the energy crisis and raised serious questions as to governmental roles in allocation systems. While some observers view energy supply constraints as potential pluses which may encourage urban concentration, most cities face short- or long-term shortages which threaten to inhibit desired growth.

Macroeconomic forces dominate the performance of the urban economy. At any point in time, a given locality's economic performance is conditioned by both national and regional growth cycles. The cities of the South and the West, the growing regions of the country, evidenced lower unemployment rates in 1973 and 1976 than the cities of the Northeast and North Central, the older, more mature economic regions. The local mix of economic activity, however, partly determines the way in which urban firms respond to business cycles. In general the cities which are most

*Gail Garfield Schwartz is Visiting Senior Fellow, Academy for Contemporary Problems.

heavily dependent upon manufacturing, in particular upon durable goods manufacture, evidence higher-than-average unemployment rates during down years and are somewhat slower to respond to improving economic conditions. Cities which specialize in providing discretionary services, such as the tourist destinations in Florida, also suffer greatly during sharp recessions.

The sweep of long-term economic forces, which tends to pull resources into new and underdeveloped areas, is, as Walt Rostow has pointed out, a natural economic phenomenon largely determined by the relative prices of resources and manufactured products. "The fifth Kondratieff upswing which began in 1972 and 1973 to create evident problems between the regions of the country . . . suddenly converted a relatively benign pattern of regional development into something of a national problem . . . because the relative rise in food and energy prices accelerated the development of a good many Sunbelt states . . . while the relative price shifts decelerated the already lower rate of expansion in the Northeast and North Central industrial states."[1]

These regional economic shifts have been accompanied by parallel (but not consequent) changes in urban structure. In all regions of our country, core cities have experienced relative declines in share of employment, even though some metropolitan areas are growing rapidly in total jobs and in total population. In San Jose, California, which has seen a huge leap in population, 65 percent of the workers commute to jobs out of the city. Boston, Philadelphia, New York, and numerous other declining-region cities have witnessed out-migration of both jobs and workers. In all regions, decentralization continues to stretch the ties between job and home as reverse- and cross-commuting become major — if not dominant — characteristics of the journey to work.

The negative consequences of these events for cities are measured in economically inefficient transportation systems, air pollution, wasteful land use, excessive costs of providing public infrastructure to serve low-density settlements, and barriers to employment of minority residents who have no access to suburban jobs because they lack transportation and/or access to suburban housing. For cities in states which deny annexation and consolidation powers, a further consequence is severe pressure on the local tax base.

The response to these negative consequences has varied from city to city and region to region, so much so that it is hard to make generalizations about urban economic development at the local level. Elected officials have extremely difficult choices to make. They must provide the services needed by residents and by business and industry, or both will vote against them—either at the polls or by "voting with their feet." On the other hand, to attract and retain business and industry in a given locality requires an appetizing array of "carrots" because sticks are of no use whatsoever. Government cannot force firms to locate anywhere.

Cities vary greatly in the success of their economic development efforts. The variation may be explained more by sociopolitical factors than by economic factors. If we could measure success along two dimensions, one the number of large enterprises, the second the degree of integration of the business, labor, and government power structures, we might find that they vary inversely and that success in economic development varies directly with the coefficient of integration. Clearly, in cities where voters evidence a strong antibusiness bias, or where fragmentation of the business community or severe labor-management antagonisms exist, local governmental efforts to implement economic development strategies will be severely hampered. This speaks to the question of public-private cooperation, about which more will be said later.

Before turning to the detailed explanation of the scope of local governmental action, let us enumerate the goals of such efforts. As commonly articulated, they are four: to increase jobs, to increase income, to bring more equity into the distribution of income, and to cushion the locality against the effects of cyclical swings. I will argue that only the first two are subject to effective local action, the equity goal being one about which local government can do very little, and the countercyclical goal being achievable only through fortuitous circumstances.

THE INSTITUTIONAL FRAMEWORK

Local government operates in the economic development arena in a complex institution framework set up by the federal and state governments. Congress, through a variety of laws, has expressed the intent to establish a spatial economic development policy. Some of this intent has been indirect, some direct.[2] That the national interest will be served by explicit, place-oriented strategies is based on at least four considerations. First, human resources are imperfectly mobile. Whether because of preference, level of capital commitment, ignorance, or all three, people are reluctant to follow job opportunities. Second, underutilized capacity, whether human or physical, constitutes a barrier to realization of full production in the aggregate. Third, federal policies do alter the competitive advantages of regions and subregions. Therefore it is something of a moral imperative for the same level of government to provide the opportunity to mitigate negative consequences. Fourth, the vast majority of governmental services are delivered through the state-local administrative structure. These services affect the ability of a locality to attract and maintain business and industry. Therefore it serves the interests of aggregate economic vitality for those levels of government to function efficiently and effectively.

The scope of local governmental action is, of course, severely limited by each state. The state must pass enabling legislation to permit cities to do any of the tasks that will be enumerated below. State legislatures determine the bonding capacity of localities and control both the tax structure and the level of taxation. Further, the executive branch of state government has budgetary and programmatic powers which influence the ability of local governments to respond to local economic conditions.

Local government, therefore, must pursue a dual strategy, one thrust directed internally to the needs of local business and one thrust directed externally. These external relations are further complicated by the fact that much assistance to local government comes directly from the federal level, without passing through state government. In its "foreign relations," therefore, the city usually must deal directly with both higher levels of government as well as participate in appropriate regional efforts. This paper will concentrate on the internal relations—that is, the scope of local governmental action with respect to the components of the local economic base.

GOVERNMENT INTERVENTION IN THE PRIVATE SECTOR

The function of local economic development activity is to intervene in the workings of the private sector to achieve a desired outcome which is not expected to occur unless the intervention is made. The types of intervention fall into two broad categories: reduction of the costs of one or more production factors and reduction of market frictions.

Reducing Costs

Real Estate Development

A primary way in which local government can reduce factor costs is by becoming a partner in real estate development or redevelopment. This role is assumed by local government in both stable economic climates and in declining ones. Since it is axiomatic that, in the aggregate, private sector action tends toward maximization of profit, it is obvious, if somewhat tautological, that governmental economic development occurs where private sector behavior does not find sufficient reward. The requisite is a high risk situation. More often than not, perceived social problems comprise part of that high risk.

The tools used by government are land assembly and write-downs, provision of infrastructure, and financing. Sometimes one of these is enough, but usually all are required. Financing is often the key to real estate development because if there is little risk, private lending institutions can afford to bankroll the entire process, including land assembly; if there is a high risk, they are unwilling to back any part of it, given more attractive alternatives for investment. The financing mechanisms include revenue bonds, mortgage guarantees and mortgage insurance, direct loans, and tax increment financing. Sometimes these mechanisms are found to be ineffectual absent a secondary market for debt instruments, but such a market can only be created at the state or federal level.[3]

Although real estate development is the most common vehicle through which local government attempts to influence economic development, government is generally hard pressed to demonstrate that a particular project will be cost effective and have a specific payoff. When payoff is measured in terms of tax revenue, most projects can demonstrate a positive net cash flow by the end of the amortization period. When the payoff is measured in jobs, the evaluation is made in terms of jobs saved as well as jobs created. The most difficult fact to prove is that the incentives offered will not merely transfer a project from one site to another, creating little, if any, net benefit.

Real estate development speaks to the goals of increasing jobs and income but seldom to the goal of equitable distribution. Financing tools, such as industrial revenue bonds, which depend on the credit rating of the firm being financed, are of little use to marginal firms, minority-owned firms, or firms in neighborhoods which lending institutions have red-lined. The inability of firms, no matter how long they have been in business, to secure expansion capital, if the neighborhood in which they are located is in transition, exists in every city in the country. Industrial and commercial red-lining in many ways is more serious than residential red-lining, since it limits the possibilities of residentially captive minorities to find any employment at all (thus limiting their ability to purchase housing). Mechanisms which are emerging to deal with this problem include linked-deposit plans, in which public deposits are used to persuade banks to make loans to business in designated areas. This is a tool which local government is obviously reluctant to use and one which can be used only when local fiscal conditions are favorable to government.

Tax Incentives

Tax incentives are a second major way in which cities can reduce the costs of doing business. Although studies of firms do not yield evidence that taxes are a significant feature in the decision to move, the research is of little practical implication because taxes are one of the few elements of overhead that is within the direct control of local government. Therefore, tax incentives are an essential economic development tool.

Tax incentives fall into three categories: general tax measures, incentives for real estate development, and tax incentives for job expansion. The variety of tax options is so great that it is beyond the scope of this paper to discuss them in detail. I would like to emphasize an important general observation: the political constraints on tax systems work directly counter to the economic objectives of the system. An extreme case is the stock transfer in New York, chosen by the legislature in preference to a gasoline tax, a toll on bridges, and other options, to close the New York City budget gap in 1975. On paper, the tax raised $250,000,000 but the brokerage firms which were to pay it started moving out of the city the day after it was legislated. Now the tax has been circumvented because it cannot be repealed, as it is an earmarked tax.

The point is that there are certain taxes that are less onerous to business than others, but these may be the most difficult ones for a legislative body to enact. In general, the taxes which inhibit investment, such as sales taxes on machinery, are to be avoided. Taxes which represent fixed costs, such as property taxes, are less conducive to business vitality in a declining economy than are corporate income taxes which rise or fall with profitability. In a rising economy, the opposite is true. Unfortunately localities have very little control over their tax system. Unfortunately, also, localities have very little understanding about how their tax system relates to their economic structure. City government can find out how much local business is paying in taxes, how this burden relates to the propensity of desired industries to remain or locate in the locality. Having discovered the facts, cities then have the choice of seeking the right to alter the local tax structure so as to more favorably influence business location decisions.

Reducing Market Friction

Government can reduce market frictions by increasing the quantity of information, by improving the quality of information, and by reducing the time required for administrative processes.

Marketing and Promotion

Marketing and promotion are potentially strong elements of any economic development program. Cities are just beginning to recognize the value of such efforts. Atlanta has established an overseas office and an office in New York City to extol the attractions of Atlanta for both manufacturing and services. Philadelphia has managed a humorous campaign using its urban hero, W.C. Fields.

In most instances, the effectiveness of a local marketing strategy is limited because it is expensive and because it is a shotgun approach. Cities need a forward-looking analysis of potential industries and businesses that stand a fair chance of operating profitably, to back up their marketing efforts. A variety of analytic techniques can be utilized in estimating economic potential, such as shift-share analysis, econometric modeling, competitive factor cost analysis, and so on. The great variety of analytic techniques is very little understood by local economic development officials. Ignoring for a moment the fact that the data available are inadequate to a full understanding of local economic potential, we must recognize that local government is not going to be able, unaided, to do the necessary analytic work to support profitable economic development activities. Local government must try to leverage 302 Planning Grants and other planning funds to maximize the value of the product. To understand the constraints on local economic potential, to be realistic about local objectives, and to balance the possible with the desirable, requires policy research of a high level of sophistication.

Administration and Regulation

Many of the tasks local government can perform to encourage business and industry are not very dramatic. They include revising regulations that inhibit expansion, such as zoning or permits. They include providing information to firms and individuals about city processes and streamlining those processes. One of the reasons that southern and western cities appear attractive to firms is that they do not have a heavy administrative overlay, and if they have the rules on the books, they manage to tailor them to fit the needs of their "client." The larger the city, the more difficult this is to do, but it is essential, particularly for the older, administratively burdened cities.

Environmental legislation is another area in which the local government is the final mediator between economic goals and conservationist goals. Because there is so much confusion respecting implementation of environment controls, local government must take the initiative in defining the tradeoff and measuring costs and benefits.

TARGETING ECONOMIC DEVELOPMENT
ACTIVITIES

The concept of targeting is not readily acceptable at the local level, but if economic development efforts are to do more than provide a few extra civil service jobs, it is essential that targeting be considered. Basic decisions must be made between equity and efficiency and between the "worst first" approach and the "creaming" approach. Moreover, a businessman's skepticism with respect to possible benefits from economic development is a necessity if a locality is to avoid costly mistakes. Cities are in a particular bind because manufacturing has been the moving target for economic development activity, and manufacturing is becoming a relatively smaller target for more hunters. The reasons that local government chases smokestacks so enthusiastically are solid ones: manufacturing has a high multiplier, it provides jobs for workers whose skills do not suit them to white collar work. Moreover, the tools available to government are more suited to construction of factories or warehouses than to encouraging white collar jobs. Service sector development requires less tangible input—a skilled, reliable labor supply, a good transportation system, some amenities that are difficult to quantify or even qualify. If local government spends all its energies on improving the governmental services which meet these requirements, its economic development efforts are in danger of becoming rather less visible than local leadership might desire. Each community must determine its own potential for diversified or specialized activities, as aggregate statistics are of no use in the specific instance.

Neighborhoods

Many city governments attempt to target economic development activities on neighborhoods which have a high incidence of poverty and/or unemployment. In general such efforts, while they may have high political payoffs, have relatively low economic payoffs. This is because industry and business perceive the risks of locating in declining or transitional neighborhoods as far too great, even given a whole range of incentives. There have been a few notable cases in which new enterprises have located in devastated inner-city areas, such as IBM in Bedfort-Stuyvesant in Brooklyn and a garment factory in Philadelphia, but so few that they prove the rule. At the local level, a more appropriate strategy is to bring people to jobs.

Another type of neighborhood economic development is commercial revitalization. Unless this is carried out with great care, it is more or less doomed to failure, since retail decline takes place because there is insufficient purchasing power in a community to support retailing, compounded often by security problems. Thus, while city governments often undertake elaborate commercial revitalization programs and such programs may be justified on other than economic grounds, they should not be looked to for major turnarounds unless the private market itself is willing to make substantial commitments.

Another concept which bears upon neighborhood development is cooperation between the public and the private sector. How does this come about? We can see it when it is there: it is there in Minneapolis, Dayton, Philadelphia, Baltimore, Kansas City, Missouri, and many others. But we really don't know of what it consists, or how to bring it about in larger, less manageable metropolises. We really don't even know what we mean by it. We do not mean that the public sector should be captive to the private market, making things happen whenever and wherever private enterprise requests. The closest approximation to a useful definition is an ongoing cooperation which does not cause government to give up its responsibilities to the general welfare but which does create a climate of trust and which illuminates both goal formation and design of strategy to meet the goals. This will bring about private sector efforts such as "five percenting," or contributions for public relations, and joint venturing for redevelopment and renovation.

THE FUTURE

The hard truth about spatially distributed economic development is that every city will not grow, and many cities must continue to decline. National economic growth will be slow for the next several years. Econometric forecasters show an average rate of change in Gross National Product of 3.8-4.5 percent through 1983 and slower rates beyond 1984. Some 15 million jobs would be required by 1985 to achieve an unemployment rate of 4 percent.[4] If, as is likely, the labor force increases faster than jobs, competition for shares will be keener but less productive.

Clearly, the chances of local governmental action being successful vary with the general economic climate of the city. The greater its current growth rate, the more likely that government intervention can increase its potential. The lower its current growth rate, the less likely various interventions will alter fundamental economic factors and the more effort will be required to make the impact felt.

The fact is that the effect of economic development policies within any given region would be far greater if efforts were not confined to existing political jurisdictions. There is no congruence between an economic region and political jurisdictions. The fundamental exchange of goods and services takes place over a geography that relates to a number of consumers, their location with respect to transportation systems, their ability to substitute other goods or services for those being offered by a particular concern, the availability of a properly trained labor force, and so on. The economic region has no relationship to village, city, county, or state boundaries, and in regions such as Buffalo is not fully limited even by international boundaries.

If the sole criterion for economic development at the subnational level were efficiency, it would obviously be far more efficient to pool efforts across functional economic regions than to pursue competitive efforts, which at best may do no more than shuffle jobs and firms around within the region. Such regions have been defined: the Bureau of Economic Analysis (BEA) has enumerated 173 regions that are relatively closed systems. The regions are aggregates of counties. Within them, any job or value-added increment benefits the entire population, with relatively little "leaking" to another economic region.

BEA regions are a logical geography over which to share the tax base. This could be accomplished through a special economic development district fund, which could collect any property, income, sales, or any other business-related tax increment resulting from new firms or relocation of firms. Disbursements from this fund could be made on a per capita basis. A small share of the incremental benefits could be reserved for the locality (city, town, or village) to offset the increased service costs, if any, generated by the firm.

From the point of view of city governments, cooperation across an economic development region would almost surely be worthwhile, since the lion's share of economic growth everywhere is going beyond the tax reach of cities.[5] From the point of view of the surrounding counties, the incentives would be the reduction of intercounty competition and the reduction of growth pressures on suburban communities. Efforts to encourage rational land use and planned, cost-effective infrastructure investment would be greatly encouraged.

Although this proposition may seem impractical, it is rational. Serious anomalies stem from the linkage of economic objectives and tax base objectives. Of the three goals most commonly associated with economic development—increasing jobs, increasing wealth, and expanding the tax base—only two are inherently economic goals. The third is a political or governance goal. Unless the third can be divorced from the first two, cities will be locked into a system of actions which in the aggregate may not contribute to region-wide or nation-wide economic growth, and which may well prove to be more costly to implement than is warranted by the net benefit created.

There are other avenues to the separation of economic and tax base issues. Various ways to restructure the fiscal system are being explored across the country. In many states, costs of local services are being picked up by state government, and the states are assuming more of the revenue-raising functions. In others, such as the Rocky Mountain states, special tax-base sharing districts are being created to help provide for the growth requirements of energy-impacted communities. Both of these approaches have the shortcoming of covering geography that is still smaller than the entire functional economic region. However, they have the virtue of moving away from the situation of locally financed services battling against a dwindling revenue base.

Local government bears heavy responsibilities and is often ill equipped by statute, by tradition, and by resources to carry them out. It would be a mistake to move too far in our enthusiam in the direction of local responsibility for economic development. While communities do well to realize the importance of economic activity to their viability, it is dangerous to expect too much in the way of local governmental efforts to alter the level and distribution of that opportunity.

The objective of cushioning a local economy against cyclical downswings is one which the locality itself, unless a stroke of luck should hit it, can do little about. The complex interindustry linkages which lure enterprises of a certain character to a locality are not amenable to manipulation by local government. Another problem that local government cannot influence very greatly is that of the distribution of economic activity, particularly the exclusion from the economic system of a vast stratum of the potential labor force. This problem applies to the hard-core unemployed, to the subemployed, and to the full-time secondary labor market--those who are relegated to temporary jobs without upward mobility. The problem is exceedingly complex, it is compounded by racism, and it is solvable only on the national level through a combination of devices including public service jobs, education, job training, and, possibly, even mobility policy. It requires massive infusions of resources and technical skills. Worse, unless real economic growth is stimulated, it will remain relatively intractable over the foreseeable future. Local government can make good use of the funds flowing from Washington for the purpose of ameliorating the conditions of these persons, but the resources of local government are too limited to permit it materially to alter the circumstances which create the problem.

Local government must get its administrative house in order, and it must provide essential services of as high a quality as possible. It can be a partner in real estate development. It can be its own public relations agent. It must assess its long-term economic potential, evaluate local barriers to realizing that potential, and seek the legislation needed to remove those barriers. It should seek an appropriate means through which to broaden the base of regional economic development. These are all formidable tasks, and they should create demand for a good number of jobs—both permanent and countercyclical.

REFERENCES

[1] Rostow, W.W. "A National Policy Towards Regional Change," Paper delivered at Western New England College, Springfield, Mass., March 1977.

[2] See Vaughan, Roger J. *The Urban Impacts of Federal Policies*, vol. 2, *Economic Development* (Santa Monica, Calif.: Rand Corp., 1977).

[3] Some states allow risk-pooling to encourage private lenders to finance small, low-credit firms, but, in general, this has not proved to be a very effective aid to such enterprises.

[4] U.S. Department of Commerce, Economic Development Administration, "Estimated Employment Expansion Required for Full Employment, 1976, 1980, and 1985—by State" (data from the Institute for Demographic and Economic Studies, New Haven, Conn., September 1976), November 1976.

[5] The exceptions are in the annexation states of the South and the West which have allowed some cities to keep up with the dispersing tax base.

The White House Conference: Findings and Recommendations

CHAPTER THIRTEEN

Note: At the Binghamton sessions in October 1977, Theodore Lane of the staff of the White House Conference gave a preview of the Conference to be held in late January 1978. That Conference has been held and the Proceedings have been published. What follows is a statement prepared by the Advisory Committee to the White House Conference.

INTRODUCTION

From Remarks at the Opening Session

A national development strategy, if we are to have one, should begin with this Conference. Growth and development will occur whether or not such an overall strategy emerges, for of course we are a Nation in constant transition.

As we begin our second 200 years, we know that the future will not resemble our past world of abundance, abundance of land, water, energy, mineral resources, forests, food. We know that things once thought free now bear price tags. We know that new resource constraints bring new dimensions to our thinking. In addition to the volume of production, we must now worry about equity in distribution. Along with both quantitative measures, we must look closely at growth's qualitative aspects.

But we know less about how to translate these perceptions into appropriate government policies.

Differential rates of growth have taught us that policies altogether macroeconomic in approach are deficient policies. A varied and changing economy calls for policies that are responsive to rates of change that differ from state to state and from worker to worker.

As a Nation, we have come rather late to serious consideration of these issues.

It is for policy guidance that we look to you. Succeed in the assignment that you take on this week and you will earn the gratitude of generations of Americans.

Honorable Juanita M. Kreps
Secretary of Commerce

From Remarks at the Closing Session

Four and one-half days ago we came together. We were strangers for the most part, and we opened a new dialog on the problems and the potentials of domestic growth. In the days that followed, we came to know one another well. We gained a new respect and tolerance for each other's views.

Over the past four days, many prominent speakers have come before our delegations in a series of dinners and luncheons and workshops to debate the issues facing this country and this Conference. And I am pleased—and frankly I am even somewhat surprised—to be able to report that this incredibly diverse group of Americans has been able to reach nearly unanimous agreement on some very basic issues.

What we have witnessed is a commonsense recognition of the need to work together. Our interdependence on every fundamental issue has overshadowed our differences.

To be sure, there have been debates.

To be sure, there have been disagreements.

But no one can deny the value of this unique and unprecedented Conference.

You have done an outstanding job in a very substantive way. This Conference is a celebration of American democracy at work.

Honorable John D. Rockefeller IV
Governor of West Virginia
Chairman of the Advisory Committee

ADVISORY COMMITTEE
RECOMMENDATIONS

The Advisory Committee to the White House Conference on Balanced National Growth and Economic Development is pleased to transmit in this volume and the appendices thereto the final report of the Conference.

The White House Conference assembled citizens from every state, representing America in all her diversity. These 500 citizens, chosen primarily by the Governors of the 50 states, struggled together over the major growth and development challenges confronting the Nation in the years ahead. In workshops, general sessions, and public forums the Conference faced head-on the complex and tough growth issues: regional divisiveness; structural unemployment; tensions in the Federal system; and conflicting energy, water, environmental, and economic objectives.

The Conference did not vote on recommendations nor did it adopt formal resolutions. Rather it was designed to encourage the replacement of rancor and divisiveness with broader understanding and a sense of common purpose in seeking answers to problems long in evolution and slow in solution. We believe that the Conference succeeded in this regard to a remarkable degree. Beyond this it spoke out with unexpected clarity and consistency on several key aspects of national development.

While the Conference did not vote, it did speak through 24 workshop reports, general session speeches, and better than 200 public forum statements. The full record is contained in this report and the appendices.

In this statement, the Advisory Committee wishes to select from the record certain suggested directions and recommendations for special consideration by the President and the public. These relate to economic growth and development issues, to improving our Federal system, and to "process" improvements that would enable this Nation to anticipate better and to address more clearly the inevitable challenges of change and growth within the framework of our economic and political traditions.

The Advisory Committee also wishes to commend the Congress and the President for convening a conference of such wide-ranging scope and for placing on its agenda contentious and perplexing questions of high national concern. Lastly, the Advisory Committee has observed, in the months following the Conference, that some of the suggested approaches are already being put into practice. They are reflected, for example, in policies found in *A Partnership to Conserve America's Communities; a National Urban Policy,* March 1978. A comprehensive analysis is also underway, within the Executive Branch, of the impact of existing Federal programs and of ways to redirect them more equitably and effectively.

GENERAL PRINCIPLES AND DIRECTIONS RELATED TO GROWTH AND DEVELOPMENT

The United States is one Nation composed of many diversified regions. No national purpose is served by setting region against region or rural areas against urban areas. National policies must recognize the diversity of the Nation's regions, states, cities, rural areas, and tribal governments. National objectives can be achieved only through a flexible policy framework which promotes overall economic and social well-being while accounting for the special characteristics of particular geographical areas.

Public policy should take into account a longer term perspective than it presently does, addressing longer term problems as well as present crises. It also should more explicitly consider the long-range impact of policy responses to immediate crises and problems.

Federal policies and programs, sometimes intentionally but more often unintentionally, have influenced the location of economic activity and population within the United States. At a minimum the likely impact of Federal activities on the well-being of people in specific places should be incorporated into the policy-making process.

Citizen involvement in the policymaking process is a proven success. All levels of government should encourage citizen involvement in shaping growth and development policy.

RECOMMENDATIONS ON GROWTH AND DEVELOPMENT ISSUES

Achieving Full Employment

The achievement of full employment is a national goal of overwhelming importance. It should be pursued primarily through efforts to create additional jobs in the private sector, with public sector jobs playing a supportive role. Controlling inflation is no less an important national objective. However, the acceptance of high unemployment as a cost of controlling inflation is neither necessary nor acceptable.

Macroeconomic Policy.

The Federal Government must provide the context of full employment through pursuing fiscal and monetary policies designed to promote the growth of a healthy economy with expanding employment opportunities.

Targeted Subnational Economic Policy.

Full employment must also be pursued through programs targeted (1) to subnational areas which experience particularly acute unemployment problems even when the national economy is healthy and (2) to particular population groups which have disproportionately high levels of unemployment—specifically minorities, youth, women, and older workers. These subnational programs targeted to areas and groups with high unemployment can reduce unemployment without creating excessive new inflationary pressures.

Emphasis on Private Sector Jobs.

The private sector is and must continue to be the primary source of new jobs. Government should continuously and consciously pursue, with the cooperation of business, methods of generating productive jobs in the private sector.

Reorientation of Public Sector Job Programs.

Public sector job programs have an important supportive, but secondary, role to play in achieving full employment. They should be designed as a flexible backup system to respond to temporary cyclical downturn or to those structurally unemployed who are unable to find employment in an expanded private sector. But public sector jobs should not be considered as a primary or permanent employment mechanism; instead such programs should emphasize the acquisition of skills transferable to private sector employment.

Jobs to People.

The primary emphasis of employment and economic development policy should be on retaining and creating jobs accessible to people where they live (jobs to people) rather than on encouraging people to move to areas where jobs are available (people to jobs).

Combating Discrimination in the Labor Market.

More effective enforcement of existing equal opportunity and affirmative action laws is essential.

Strengthening Local Economies Through Economic Development

Economic development of distressed areas should be a primary national objective.

Targeting.

Federal and state economic and community development funds should be targeted on distressed places, regardless of region, whether they be central cities, suburbs, rural areas or areas impacted by rapid and disorderly economic growth.

Incentives for Private Sector Development.

A variety of incentives—tax credits and deductions, direct loans and loan guarantees, and grants—should be provided to attract private sector economic activity to distressed areas.

Federal Procurement and Facility Location.

Federal and state governments have in the past too frequently exacerbated economic distress through facility location decisions. Wherever possible, Federal facility location and procurement policies should aid distressed areas.

Reducing the Fiscal Problems of Local Governments

Federal and state governments have a responsibility to help reduce the fiscal problems of local governments and to reduce disparities in the fiscal capacity of local governments.

Reassignment of Fiscal Functions.

The Federal Government should assume greater responsibility for financing welfare and medicaid, thereby removing an onerous fiscal burden from state and county governments (and some cities). In return, state governments should assume a greater portion of the cost of local public education, thereby removing an onerous fiscal burden from local governments.

Increased State Fiscal Assistance.

States should assume greater responsibility for the fiscal conditions of their local governments through increased aid targeted to fiscally distressed local governments.

Tax Base Sharing.

Metropolitan areas should adopt tax base sharing as a means of providing assistance to fiscally hard-pressed local governments within those areas and as a means of reducing disparities in fiscal capacity among local governments. States have the primary responsibility for bringing this about.

Credit Guarantees.

The Federal Government should provide credit guarantees, under very limited conditions and strict supervision, to local governments facing severe debt problems.

Need for a National Energy Policy

National economic development and employment goals cannot be met without a corresponding energy policy. The essential components of such a policy are:

1. The conservation of energy resources;
2. The provision of incentives for energy production, including development of new energy sources and reduced dependence on foreign energy sources.

RECOMMENDATIONS FOR IMPROVING THE FEDERAL SYSTEM

Fair and Flexible Federalism

The Federal Government must begin to play a more sensitive role in the Federal system. It should set national objectives, but at the same time, should recognize the great diversity among regions, states and localities. Federal programs should be flexible enough to respond to this diversity, permitting states and localities to pursue national objectives—and their own as well—in ways which are appropriate to local conditions and needs.

Greater Decentralization Within the Federal System.

There is a need for greater decentralization, particularly in the administration of federally funded programs, within the Federal system. Specifically, the Federal Government should move toward a system that would permit, whenever possible, greater local discretion and evaluation through performance standards rather than through lengthy application procedures and rigid administrative guidelines.

Assumption of Greater Responsibility by State Governments.

State governments, for their part, should assume greater responsibility for:

1. Improving state and local government structure;
2. Alleviating the fiscal problems of their local governments;
3. Managing growth and decline within the state.

Greater Federal Assumption of Welfare and Medicaid; Greater State Assumption of Education Costs.

Fair and flexible federalism requires a reassignment among levels of government of the responsibility for financing various functions. In particular, the Federal Government should assume a greater portion of the cost of public assistance and medicaid programs, while the state government should assume a greater portion of the state-local cost of elementary and secondary education.

Improving the Structure of State and Local Government

State and local governments must improve their structures and operations.

Areawide Cooperation and Tax Base Sharing.

State government has the primary responsibility for rationalizing and reforming local government structure. It should take the lead in bringing about greater areawide cooperation and fiscal equity, both in metropolitan and regional areas, through devices such as tax base sharing.

Capacity Building.

State and local governments should improve their capacity to plan for and manage growth through modernizing governmental structure, personnel systems, and administrative operations, through instituting state and local growth policy processes, and through adopting growth policies and strategies.

Federal Incentives for State and Local Action.

The Federal Government should provide encouragement and inducements for state governments to assume a more responsible role in coping with the problems of their local governments in modernizing governmental structure, in reforming inequitable state and local revenue systems and expenditure patterns, and in developing revitalization strategies and a capacity to manage growth.

Multistate Regional Institutions.

Effective multistate regional arrangements are necessary for problems transcending state boundaries. Regional institutions, consisting of Federal, state, and local officials and private sector representatives, should provide the opportunity for shaping development plans for the region.

Creating an Effective Private-Public Sector Partnership

The private sector must be brought into a creative and cooperative partnership with Federal, state and local governments if we are to achieve our national objectives. This partnership should be based on the recognition that the key to long-term economic growth lies in the creation of permanent private sector jobs. The private sector—including private citizens and nonprofit groups—must be involved at all levels of government in the design and implementation of economic development and employment programs.

RECOMMENDATIONS FOR A NATIONAL GROWTH AND DEVELOPMENT POLICY PROCESS

Inadequacy of Existing Policy Processes and Structure

Perhaps the clearest and most important message of the Conference was a pervasive sense that the Nation and its governmental institutions—particularly the Federal Government—must enhance and more fully utilize their capacities to address the long-term growth and development challenges that lie ahead. In particular, the Conference pointed to these deficiencies:

1. Inadequate ability to anticipate future problems and trends;
2. Inadequate attention given to mid- and long-range issues (as opposed to short-term crises which demand immediate responses), and to the mid- and long-term implications of responses to immediate problems;
3. Inadequate coordination among government programs, policies, and agencies;

4. Inadequate coordination among the levels of government within the Federal system;
5. Inadequate recognition of possible conflicts among multiple national objectives with the resultant inability to make careful trade-offs;
6. Insensitivity and lack of responsiveness of government as evidenced by over-detailed regulations and the pervasiveness of red tape.

Creation of a National Growth Policy Process

A national growth policy process involving the private as well as the public sector, all levels of government, and citizen input is called for in order to improve the Nation's policy processes. The process should have several components:

Growth Meetings and Forums.

Many states currently have some form of growth forum, commission, or process. These state growth processes have proven quite successful, and other states should be encouraged to adopt them. The goal should be regular annual or biennial meetings at the state, regional, and national levels bringing together diverse elements to consider growth policy issues. These meetings should include an opportunity for the public to participate through a public forum such as that which occurred at the White House Conference.

A Federal Growth Policy Unit.

There should be established, within the Federal Government, an organizational unit responsible for providing advice to the President and the Nation on mid- to long-range growth and development issues facing the Nation.

A Growth Policy Process.

The above mentioned unit should be concerned with:

1. Clarification of national goals;
2. Improving forecasting and projection capabilities for national and subnational areas to provide a better basis for understanding the

implications of future growth and development changes and policies required to address them;

3. Analyzing the impact of existing and proposed alternative policies on growth and development objectives, including an analysis of their impact on regions, central cities, rural areas, and other important categories;

4. Identifying conflicts among objectives and programs and analyzing possible trade-offs among them;

5. Coordinating Federal activities as they relate to national growth objectives. This would include responsibility for the coordination and production of periodic reports on national growth and development such as the existing separate reports mandated for urban policy and rural development.

Congressional Organization for Growth Policy.

The fragmented processes through which Congress currently addresses national growth policy issues make coherent and consistent policymaking difficult, particularly for mid- to long-range issues. Congress should develop the capability, through reorganization or other means, to address growth policy issues more effectively and to make available to its members better information related to these issues.

**Briefing for members of the Advisory
Committee at the White House.**

INDEX

189